Arbaeen
The Walk

Mohammed Al-Hilli

Copyright © 2017 by Mohammed Al-Hilli

All rights reserved. This book or any portion thereof may not be reproduced or used in any manner whatsoever without the express written permission of the publisher except for the use of brief quotations in a book review.

First Printing, 2017

ISBN 978-1-939420-03-9

English translation of the Quranic verses taken from *The Qur'ān: With a Phrase-by-Phrase English Translation*, ICAS Press: London 2003 (Third Revised Edition 2009)

All enquiries and feedback to sheikh@alhilli.net
Address: 4 Dalston Gardens, Stanmore, HA7 1BU

Published by:

Taqwa Media
Monmouth Junction, NJ
www.taqwamedia.com

IN THE NAME OF ALLAH,
THE MOST COMPASSIONATE THE MOST MERCIFUL

ذٰلِكَ الَّذي يُبَشِّرُ اللَّهُ عِبادَهُ الَّذينَ آمَنوا وَعَمِلُوا الصّالِحاتِ ۗ
قُل لا أَسأَلُكُم عَلَيهِ أَجرًا إِلَّا المَوَدَّةَ فِي القُربىٰ

'That is the good news Allah gives to His servants who have faith and do righteous deeds! *Say*, 'I do not ask you any reward for it except love of my family.'

Holy Qur'an (42:23)

Arabic Colophons used in this book:

Subhanahu Wata'ala
Glorified and Exalted
(used immediately after referring to God the Almighty)

Sallalahu Alayhi wa alihi wa Salaam
May Allah's peace and blessings be upon him and his progeny
(used immediately after referring to the Prophet Mohammad)

Alayhi al-Salaam
May Allah bless him
(used immediately after referring to a single Imam or Prophet)

Alayha al-Salaam
May Allah bless her
(used immediately after referring to an honourable female)

Alayhum al-Salaam
May Allah bless them
(used immediately after referring to a group of the Imams or Prophets)

Ajal Allah farajahu al-Sharif
May Allah hasten his reappearance
(used immediately after referring to Imam Al-Mahdi)

Quddisa Sirroh
May his soul be blessed
(used immediately after referring to a single deceased and respected scholar)

Table of Contents

Dedication 7
Preface 9
The Merits of the Ziyarah of Imam Hussain 15
The Significance of Number 40 21
The Evidence for the Arbaeen Ziyarah 25
The Historical Significance of the 20th of Safar 31
The Benefit of the Arbaeen Walk 37
The Walk to Karbala: Background and Philosophy 55
The Reward of Walking Barefoot for Ziyarah 67
Etiquettes of the Walk 71
Useful Tips for the Walk from Najaf to Karbala 81
Recommendations for the Arbaeen Walk 85
Personal Experiences of the Walk to Karbala 89
Etiquettes of Ziyarah 107
Brief Commentary on Ziyarat Al-Arbaeen 115
The Meaning of Labbayk Ya Hussain 137
Appendix 143
Bibliography 149
About the Author 153
Notes 154

Dedication

To the one who witnessed the tragedies of her grandfather, father, mother, and brothers.

To the one who accompanied her brothers and painfully went through the sorrows of Karbala.

To the one who lost her sons, brothers, nephews, and family members all within a few hours!

To the one who saw the enemy of God sit on the chest of her brother before beheading him!

To the one who protected and looked after the orphans and the widows.

To the one who was beaten, paraded, and taken as captive from one city to another.

To the one who shook the kingdom of the tyrants with her eloquence, valour, and vision.

To the one whom patience itself was humbled before her.

To the one who returned forty days after the martyrdom of her family to the land of the Karbala.

To the one who continues to inspire millions with her eternal legacy.

To the ornament of her father, Zainab bint Ali ﷺ, I dedicate this work, seeking her intercession on the day of reckoning.

Preface

The Walk of the Free, the Journey of Liberation. The Steps to Paradise, the Path of Loyalty and the Movement to God.

Walking for love, devotion and a willingness to sacrifice for the grandson of the Prophet, Imam Hussain ﷺ, are the ruling characteristics of the multi-million people walk to Karbala since the year 2003.

Drawing people from across the world, including different denominations and backgrounds, the Arbaeen walk has been declared as the world's largest pilgrimage.[1] The commemoration marks the anniversary of the 40th day after Ashura, the date of the martyrdom of Imam Hussain, his family, and companions in the land of Karbala in 680AD. Despite little media focus and coverage, the annual walk by millions grows stronger each year.

This mass pilgrimage has its roots across history, despite the attempts of tyrants and governments to eradicate it. Historical records provide us with in-depth descriptions of intimidation, harassment, and punishment for those who undertook the journey towards Karbala. This includes the Abbasid Caliph Al-Mutawakil (d. 861), who severed the hands and feet of those who performed the visitation of Imam Hussain ﷺ.

During the despotic rule of the Baathists in Iraq, people walked from across the country to Karbala, utilising farms and lesser known avenues. This meant walking at night, or through small avenues and streets so as not to be spotted by government agents and spies. Despite this many were arrested or executed. A particularly poignant incident occurred in December 1976, when the Baathist security apparatus brutally showered the pilgrims with bullets - killing many and injuring several more.

Following the collapse of the regime in 2003, the number of people walking to Karbala increased, despite the worsening security situation. The continuous bombings, kidnapping, and assassinations did not dissuade people, and they continued flocking towards the city of Imam Hussain ﷺ.

1https://www.washingtonpost.com/news/monkey-cage/wp/2016/11/21/shiites-are-participating-in-the-worlds-largest-pilgrimage-today-heres-how-they-view-the-world/?utm_term=.d3a86dded617 accessed 2 June 2017

Estimates show that, by 2014, over 19 million people from 40 countries of the world participated in the Arbaeen walk.[2] In 2015, Iraqi state-run media placed the figure at 22 million. The same figure was also registered for the year 2016. These figures usually include those who travel from various countries around the world, including Iran, the Middle East, Europe and America, Pakistan and India. Figures of such participation from outside Iraq have ranged from 750,000 to 2 million.

The vivid remembrance and the increasing numbers of visitors to this blessed place were predicted by the sister of Imam Hussain ﷺ, Lady Zainab bint Ali ﷺ. In a narration, it is reported that she said to Imam Ali ibn Hussain ﷺ:

'Do not be sad for what you see. It is, by Allah I swear, only the announcement that Almighty Allah has already made to your grandfather and father. Allah has certainly made a covenant with some people, who are not known by the tyrants on this earth but they are well known by the inhabitants of the Heavens, that they shall gather these severed organs and these bloodstained bodies to bury them. They shall also hoist in this land, al-Taff, a flag on the tomb of your father the Master of the Martyrs. Throughout days and ages, the mark of this tomb shall never be obliterated and its figure shall not be blotted out. Nevertheless, the heads of atheism and the spreaders of deviation shall exert all efforts for obliterating it, yet this shall make it more and more elevated instead.'[3]

Noticeably, the Arbaeen walk is not specific to any age group, gender, or denomination. Men, women, children, and elderly walk for days towards the city of Karbala, braving terrorism, the weather, and living conditions to make sure they participate. They are served regularly by approximately two thousand *mawkibs* (areas of rest, food, and sleep), which are set up by tribes and volunteers throughout the different roads that lead to the city. Whilst many start the walk from the city of Najaf, thousands choose longer journeys and start from places such as Baghdad and Basra (500km away from Karbala).

Over the years, several terrorists have attempted to cause maximum loss of life and destruction by either planting bombs or blowing themselves up. Many were captured or were unsuccessful, and the walk

---

2. http://www.independent.co.uk/news/world/middle-east/on-of-the-worlds-biggest-and-most-dangerous-pilgrimages-is-underway-9882702.html
3 Kamil Al-Ziyarat, p.447

has largely been trouble free and fully safe thus far. This divine protection of the pilgrims is an indication of the special position that Imam Hussain occupies in the eyes of Allah ﷻ. Visitors are reminded of the Quranic verse:

وَجَعَلَنِي مُبَارَكًا أَيْنَ مَا كُنْتُ

'...and he made me blessed wherever I am..'[4]

Indeed, the blessed nature of the Imam ؏ has now extended far and wide and can be felt by the visitor heading towards the city of martyrs. This includes the power of association and loyalty to the path of the Imam and seeking to be guided and inspired by his sacrifice and eternal message. Truly, as the Prophet Mohammad ﷺ is narrated to have said:

'Surely Hussain is the lantern of guidance and the ship of salvation.'

The Almighty ﷻ has emphasised the importance of upholding the signs that lead to Him, and increase His remembrance. One such direction is in the Holy Qur'an:

ذٰلِكَ وَمَن يُعَظِّم شَعَائِرَ اللَّهِ فَإِنَّها مِن تَقْوَى الْقُلُوبِ

'That. And whoever venerates the sacraments of Allah – indeed that arises from the God-wariness of hearts.[5]'

The Walk of Arbaeen is undoubtedly one of the signs of God, whereby millions express their love and loyalty to a man who is beloved to the Almighty, and gave everything for His sake. One may ask; why such a display of love and devotion? Why, when faced with threats, do people flock towards Karbala - completely unfazed by what could happen to them?

For many, from the moment they were introduced to the values and principles which were magnificently demonstrated on the plains of Karbala 1400 years ago, they felt a sense of connection and deep reverence. In Hussain, they find faith, truth, sacrifice, justice, honour,

---

[4] Holy Qur'an (19:31)
[5] Holy Qur'an (22:32)

dignity, altruism, spirituality, sincerity, tranquillity, and salvation. That is why Imam Hussain continues to be one of the world's greatest super powers, inspiring hundreds of millions annually to become better human beings.

The walk to Karbala does not only take place during the commemoration of the 40th. During Ashura (10th Muharram), 15th Shaban, and Thursday nights, it is common to see the city of Karbala filled with visitors. Yet, Arbaeen is unique. Not only do the millions of visitors seek to establish their loyalty with Imam Hussain ﷺ, but they walk to honour the sacrifice of the caravan of the captives, who were paraded from one city to another yet never surrendered or gave up. Narrations suggest they eventually returned to Karbala on 20th Safar, 40 days after the Day of Ashura.

The emphasis to uphold the remembrance of Imam Hussain ﷺ and to connect emotionally with the tragedy, including the highlighting of the immense reward of walking to his shrine, has been encouraged by the Ahlulbayt ﷺ. This is not for ritualistic purposes though. Rather, for centuries, such commemoration seeks to establish the tenets of Islamic teachings and bring people closer to Allah ﷻ. The spirit of mourning for Ashura fulfils the objective of Islamic teachings - complete submission to God and the obedience of His commands.

Having been blessed to undertake the walk to Karbala during Arbaeen for several years, I decided to work on a publication that highlights the background, philosophy, and merits of undertaking this act of devotion. A few personal experiences were gathered from those who undertook the walk over the past few years. It is hoped the book will inspire those who have not yet discovered this beautiful display of loyalty to do so soon and provide insight to others around the world on what is now a tremendous phenomenon.

I would like to thank Zuhair Rattansi for the design of the front and back covers as well as Reshma Jaffrey for the relentless editing of this book. May Allah ﷻ reward them abundantly. I would also like to thank all those who supported this work through various ways, including the many brothers and sisters who sent their experiences of the walk.

May Allah ﷻ grant us all the blessing to be amongst the regular visitors of Imam Hussain ؑ in Karbala, especially during the walk of Arbaeen, and bestow upon us the opportunity to receive the intercession of the Ahlulbayt ؑ in the hereafter.

Mohammed Al-Hilli
Holy City of Najaf
7th Dhulhijja 1438
29th August 2017

Chapter 1:

The Merits of the Ziyarah of Imam Hussain ﷺ

The Ziyarah of Imam Hussain ﷺ has always featured heavily in the teachings of the Ahlulbayt. To visit the third Holy Imam is to obey a command of Allah ﷻ where he asks us to display love and loyalty towards the pure progeny.[6] Human beings have a natural tendency to follow those who inspire them, hence visiting Imam Hussain ﷺ is the perfect way to show their connection to him in a practical way as well as fulfil their desire to follow in the footsteps of the grandson of the Prophet. Upon doing a detailed analysis of the numerous narrations we can find over 100 benefits of this Ziyarah - both in this world and the hereafter. Some of these include:

- **Extensive rewards in the hereafter**

Imam Sadiq ﷺ is reported to have said:

'I heard my father ask one of his followers, who had inquired about the Ziyarat of Imam Hussain ﷺ, "To whose Ziyarat are you going and whose pleasure do you seek by this Ziyarat?" He replied, "Allah, the blessed and exalted." My father said: One who prays one prayer at the grave of Imam Hussain ﷺ seeking proximity with Allah will meet Him on Judgment Day shining so brightly that his light will cover everything that looks at them. Allah will honour one who performs the Ziyarat of Imam Hussain ﷺ and He will prevent Hellfire from touching him. He will not be prevented from coming to Pool of Kawther and no one will precede him. Imam Ali ﷺ will be standing by the Pool and will shake his hands and serve water to him. Then he will enter his dwellings in Paradise accompanied by an angel appointed by Imam Ali ﷺ who

---

[6] '..Say, 'I do not ask you any reward for it except love of my family.' Holy Qur'an (42:23)

will order the Sirat Bridge to lower itself before him and order Hellfire not to touch him till he passes over it.'[7]

- **Prayers of the angels:**

Imam Sadiq is reported to have said:

'There are four thousand angels by the grave of Imam Hussain, dishevelled and covered with dust. They will cry over him until Judgment Day. Their chief is an angel named Mansur. These angels welcome all who come to the Ziyarat of Imam Hussain and accompany them when they bid farewell to Imam Hussain, visit them if they become ill and pray for them at their funerals when they die and seek forgiveness for them after their death.'[8]

- **Honoured by Allah**

Imam Sadiq:

'All will wish on Judgment Day to be among the visitors of Imam Hussain, because they will see the way in which the visitor of Imam Hussain is honoured and treated by the Almighty Allah.'[9]

- **Forgiveness of sins**

Imam Kadhim:

'Allah will forgive all past and future sins of one who performs the Ziyarat of Imam Hussain with recognition of his rights.'[10]

- **Being with the Ahlulbayt in Paradise**

Imam Sadiq:

'On Judgment Day, an announcer will call out, "Where are the visitors of Hussain bin Ali?" Many people, who cannot be counted by anyone other than

---

[7] Kamil Al-Ziyarat, p. 121
[8] Kamil Al-Ziyarat, p. 118
[9] ibid, p. 133
[10] ibid, p. 135

the Almighty Allah, will come forward. Then Allah will ask them, "What impelled you to perform the Ziyarat of Hussain ؑ?

They will reply, "O Lord! We went to him for our love for Allah's Messenger and love for Ali and Fatima and to sympathize with him for all that which was committed against him." They will be told, "Here are Mohammad, Ali Fatima, Hasan and Hussain ؑ; join them, for you will be with them at their stage in Paradise. Follow the standard of Allah's Messenger ﷺ." So, they will go to the standard of Allah's Messenger ﷺ, which will be held by Ali ؑ; they will remain under it, before it, to its right, to its left and behind it, until all of them enter Paradise.'[11]

- **Brilliant rewards**

Imam Baqir ؑ:

"If people knew the reward for performing the Ziyarat of Imam Hussain ؑ, their souls would leave their bodies in remorse and they would die longing for it."

I asked, "What is the reward for going to his Ziyarat?" Imam ؑ replied: Allah will record the reward of a thousand accepted Hajjs, a thousand accepted Umrahs, a thousand martyrs of Badr, fasting of a thousand people, a thousand accepted prostrations and the reward of freeing a thousand slaves in the way of Allah for one who goes to the Ziyarat of Imam Hussain ؑ longing for him. He will be protected for a whole year from every calamity, the least of which is Shaitan. And Allah will appoint a noble angel to protect him from front, behind, right, left, above and below.

If he dies that year, angels of divine mercy will be present with him, bathe and shroud him and seek forgiveness for him. They will also follow him till the grave and widen it as far as the eye can see and Allah will keep him safe from the squeeze of the grave and from fear of angels, Munkar and Nakeer. A door will also be opened from his grave to Paradise. On Judgment Day, scroll of deeds will be given in his right hand and he will shine with a light, which illuminates from the east to west. And an announcer will call out, "He is one who performed the Ziyarat of Imam Hussain ؑ with enthusiasm." After that no one will remain on Judgment Day who will not wish he had also performed the Ziyarat of Imam Hussain ؑ.'[12]

---

[11] ibid, p. 137
[12] Kamil Al-Ziyarat, p. 139

- **Prolongs life and increases sustenance**

Imam Baqir ﷺ:

'Order our Shias to visit the grave of Imam Hussain ﷺ, because his Ziyarat increases sustenance, prolongs life and keeps afflictions away.'[13]

- **Reward of Hajj and Umrah**

'I (the narrator) said to Imam Sadiq ﷺ, "May I be sacrificed on you, I cannot afford to go to Hajj every year."

Imam ﷺ replied:

'If you ever wanted to go to the Hajj but could not afford it, go to the Ziyarat of Imam Hussain ﷺ, for indeed it will be recorded as a Hajj for you. And if you ever wanted to go for Umrah but could not afford it, go to the Ziyarat of Imam Hussain ﷺ, for indeed it will be recorded as an Umrah for you.'[14]

- **Intercession for others**

Imam Sadiq ﷺ:

'On Judgment Day, an announcer will announce, "Where are the Shia of Aale Mohammad ﷺ?" A group of people whose number cannot be counted except by the Almighty Allah, will stand up and separate from the people. Then an announcer will announce, "Where are the visitors of the grave of Imam Hussain ﷺ?"
A large group of people will stand up. They will be told, "Take the hand of whoever you like and take him to Paradise with you." They will take whoever they like to Paradise to such an extent that a person will say to one of them, "O so and so! Don't you remember me? I stood up for you once as a mark of respect." So, the visitor will take him to Paradise without being stopped.'[15]

---

[13] ibid, p. 143
[14] ibid, p. 146. This is of course after the obligatory hajj is performed
[15] ibid, p. 155

- Relief from distress and grief

Imam Baqir ؏:

'Imam Hussain ؏ of Karbala was slain while he was oppressed, distressed, thirsty and aggrieved. It is indeed fitting that every aggrieved, distressed, sinful, saddened, thirsty and ill person who goes to his Ziyarat and prays near his grave, seeks proximity to Allah through him, will have his grief removed and Allah will fulfil his needs, forgive his sins, prolong his life and increase his sustenance. "So take a lesson, O those who have insight!"[16]

- An important narration on the importance of Ziyarah

Mua'wiya ibn Wahab, a faithful and loyal companion of the Imam, narrates he heard Imam Sadiq say in his prostration:

'Lord! You are the One Who chose us to receive Your bliss, promised us to intercede, granted us the knowledge of what passed and of what remains, made the hearts of some people lean towards us: I invoke You to forgive me and my brethren and those who visit the grave-site of my grandfather Hussain, those who spend their wealth and exhaust themselves out of their desire to express their devotion to us, hoping to earn the rewards which You have for all those who maintain their link with us, and because of the pleasure they bring to Your Prophet, and out of their response to our own order to do so. Reward them for having vexed our enemy as they sought Your Pleasure. Do reward them, O Lord, on our behalf, and grant them sustenance during the night and the day, and be generous to their families and offspring, those who succeed them in doing such good deeds. Be their Friend; ward off from them the evil of all stubborn tyrants, all those from among Your creatures. Protect their weak from the evil of the mighty ones, be they demons, humans, or jinns. And grant them the best of what they aspire as they estrange themselves from their homelands, and for preferring us to their sons, families, and kinsfolk.

Lord! Our enemies find fault with their going out to visit our shrines, yet it does not stop them from doing so, unlike those who oppose us. Lord! Have mercy on the faces transformed by the heat of the sun. Have mercy on the cheeks that

---

[16] Kamil Al-Ziyarat, p. 156

touch the grave of Abu `Abdillah, Al-Hussain. Have mercy on the eyes that weep out of kindness to us. Have mercy on the hearts that are grieved on our account and are fired with passion for us. And have mercy on those who mourn us. Lord! I implore You to be the Custodian of these souls and bodies till You bring them to the Pool [of Kawther] on the Day of the great thirst.'

When Mua'wiya ibn Wahab regarded this supplication as giving "too much" for those who visit the gravesite of Imam Hussain ﷺ, Imam Sadiq said to him, "Those in the heavens who supplicate for those who visit Hussain's gravesite are more numerous than those who do so on earth."[17]

---

[17] ibid, p. 116

Chapter 2:

The Significance of Number 40

An examination of the holy Qur'an and narrations from the Prophet and his progeny reveals an emphasis on the number 40. This number is referred to four times in the holy book:

وَإِذ واعَدنا موسىٰ أَربَعينَ لَيلَةً

'And when We made an appointment with Moses for forty nights...'[18]

وَواعَدنا موسىٰ ثَلاثينَ لَيلَةً وَأَتمَمناها بِعَشرٍ فَتَمَّ ميقاتُ رَبِّهِ أَربَعينَ لَيلَةً

'And We made an appointment with Moses for thirty nights, and completed them with ten [more]; thus, the trust of his Lord was completed in forty nights.'[19]

وَوَصَّينَا الإِنسانَ بِوالِدَيهِ إِحسانًا ۖ حَمَلَتهُ أُمُّهُ كُرهًا وَوَضَعَتهُ كُرهًا ۖ وَحَملُهُ وَفِصالُهُ ثَلاثونَ شَهرًا ۚ حَتّىٰ إِذا بَلَغَ أَشُدَّهُ وَبَلَغَ أَربَعينَ سَنَةً

'We have enjoined man to be kind to his parents. His mother has carried him in travail, and bore him in travail, and his gestation and weaning take thirty months. When he comes of age and reaches forty years...'[20]

فَإِنَّها مُحَرَّمَةٌ عَلَيهِم ۛ أَربَعينَ سَنَةً ۛ يَتيهونَ فِي الأَرضِ

'It shall be forbidden them for forty years: they shall wander about in the earth.'[21]

Such references in the holy Qur'an cannot be coincidental and therefore indicate the significance of this number.

---

[18] Holy Qur'an (2:51)
[19] Holy Qur'an (7:142)
[20] Holy Qur'an (46:15)
[21] Holy Qur'an (5:26)

Similarly, the narrations from the Ahlulbayt elucidate this point further:

1. **Memorisation of 40 hadiths**

It is narrated that the Prophet Mohammad ﷺ said:

'Whomsoever from my ummah memorises 40 hadiths, which they will benefit from, will be resurrected by Allah on the day of judgement as a knowledgeable scholar.'[22]

2. **Not seeking repentance until age of 40**

The Prophet ﷺ is narrated to have mentioned:

'If a person reaches the age of 40 and does not seek repentance, Satan will wipe over the face and hands and say: surely a face that will not succeed.'[23]

3. **The dua of forty people**

Imam Al-Sadiq ؏ is narrated to have said:

'If forty people gather together and supplicate to Allah for a (fulfilment) of deeds, the Almighty will respond to them.'[24]

4. **40 believers and the funeral**

Imam Al-Sadiq ؏:

'When a believer dies, 40 believers should attend his funeral and say: 'O Allah, we do not know anything but good about him, and You are more knowledgeable about him than us.' Upon this, Allah will reply: 'I have accepted your witnessing and have forgiven him what I know and you do not.'[25]

---

[22] Al-Kafi, vol.1, p.49
[23] Tabaqat al-Shaf'ya al-Kubra, vol.1, p.331
[24] Wasa'il Al-Shia, vol.7, p.103
[25] Man la Yahthrahu Al-faqih, vol.1, p.165

5. Praying for 40 believers before one's self

Imam Sadiq ؑ:

'Whomsoever remembers 40 believers in their supplication before remembering themselves will have their dua answered (by Allah).'[26]

6. Sprinkling water on the grave for 40 days

It is narrated that Mohammad ibn Al-Walid was asked about the grave of Yunus ibn Yaqub by the graveyard caretaker:

'Who is buried in this grave? For Ali ibn Musa Al-Ridha ؑ commanded me to water the grave for forty months or forty days continuously.'[27]

7. Sincerity for 40 days

Imam Baqir ؑ:

'Whoever displays sincerity towards Allah for 40 days Allah will grant him zuhd (asceticism) in this world...and will place wisdom in their hearts and make it ooze from their tongues.'[28]

8. Narrations point to the length of the kingdom of Prophet Dawood ؑ to be 40 years.[29]

The emphasis on the number 40 is such that one scholar, Allamah Al-Tehrani, in his book *'Al-Dharee'a'*, lists the names of 77 books compiled from the 4th century until the 14th century, which have the name 'Arbaeen'. These books cover a range of areas, such as divine leadership (Imamat), rulings, spirituality, and ethics.[30]

---

[26] Wasa'il Al-Shia, vol. 4, p.332
[27] Wasa'il Al-Shia, vol.2, p.860
[28] Bihar Al-Anwar, vol.67, p.144
[29] ibid, vol.16, p.311
[30] Al-Dharee'a, vol.1, p.409

The link between Imam Hussain ﷺ and the number 40

Several narrations have pointed to a connection:

1. One of the signs of believers is the Arbaeen Ziyarah

Imam Hasan Askari ﷺ is narrated to have said:

'The signs of a believer are five: performing 51 Rokats a day, the Arbaeen Ziyarah, wearing a ring on the right hand, prostration on soil and the proclaiming of Bismillah loudly (in prayer).'[31]

2. The water drying at his grave after 40 days

The historian Ibn Kathir narrates:

'Water was running over the grave of Hussain ﷺ so that it is concealed. After 40 days, the water dried'. A Bedouin from Bani Asad thereafter attended the grave and took parts of the soil whilst weeping. He then said:

'May my father and mother be scarified for you; how pure you are and how your soil is so fragranced.'[32]

3. The weeping of the heavens and earth for 40 days

Imam Sadiq ﷺ is narrated to have said:

'O Zurara, the heaven wept blood for Hussain for 40 days, the earth wept for 40 days in darkness, the sun wept for 40 days through an eclipse, the mountains crumbled and exploded, the angels cried for 40 days over Imam Hussain ﷺ...'[33]

---

[31] Bihar Al-Anwar, vol.98, p.329
[32] Al-Bidya wal Nihaya, vol.8, p.205
[33] Kamil Al-Ziyarat, p.88

Chapter 3:

The Evidence for the Arbaeen Ziyarah

Scholars from the school of Ahlulbayt ؏ have presented several discussions pointing towards the legitimacy and excellence of the Arbaeen Ziyarah of Imam Hussain ؏. Broadly, these are divided into four main areas:

The narrations

A. The Imam Askari ؏ narration

The 11th holy Imam of the Ahlulbayt, Imam Hasan Askari ؏, is narrated to have said:

'The signs of a believer are five: performing 51 Rokats a day, the Arbaeen Ziyarah, wearing a ring on the right hand, prostration on soil and the proclaiming of Bismillah loudly (in prayer).'[34]

From this narration, the words of the Imam, *'Ziyarat Al-Arbaeen'* have been interpreted as the visitation of Imam Hussain ؏ on 20th Safar, 40 days after his martyrdom on the 10th Muharram. We can infer this from the following:

1. The Arabic word 'Arbaeen' has been pre-fixed with the alif and lam, denoting the identification of a known matter. This is referred to as the *'Lam Al-Ahd Al-Thuhni'*, meaning the prefix of the word is understood and known to the listener and it identifies a known aspect. This is like the word *'Al-Rasul'* (apostle) in the following Quranic verse:

---

[34] Misbah Al-Mutahajid, p.788. Tahdhib Al-Ahkam, vol.6, p.52

فَعَصَىٰ فِرْعَوْنُ الرَّسُولَ فَأَخَذْنَاهُ أَخْذًا وَبِيلًا

'But Pharaoh disobeyed the apostle; so We seized him with a terrible seizing.'[35]

Clearly 'the' in the verse identifies Musa ؈ as the apostle sent by Allah ﷻ. Hence, by deduction, the way the word Arbaeen is understood reflects what is usually associated with it, and that is the 40th of Imam Hussain ؈. This is especially the case when we discuss the context of these five characteristics, given they are part of the attributes of a 'believer'.

2. The word 'believer' in the Shia heritage of narrations usually denotes a follower of Ahlulbayt ؈. This has been affirmed in the jurisprudential works on Shia jurists for centuries. Ayatollah Ali Sistani states:

'At the same time we must understand that a Muslim and a 'believer' have been distinguished in the words of Ahlulbayt ؈, where a 'believer' is used to refer to Shias only...'[36]

3. The political situation at the time of Imam Askari ؈ was such that the Abbasid rulers sought desperately to erase the remembrance of Imam Hussain ؈ and prohibit people from visiting his grave. Historians have documented how the likes of Al-Mutawakil destroyed the grave and its surroundings, punishing those who made the journey to visit it.

The famous historian Al-Tabari narrates:

'In year 236AH, Al-Mutawakil[37] ordered the destruction of Hussain ibn Ali's grave. He also destroyed the houses adjacent to the grave. The area was then dug out and water was poured into it. People were prevented from visitation.'[38]

---

[35] Holy Qur'an (73:16)
[36] Minhaj Al-Saleehen, vol.1, ruling.1259

On this basis and given the difficult situation facing the Shia, the Imams wanted to keep the focus on the visitation and encourage this practice to continue. Other narrations point to Imam Askari ؑ asking others to perform the Ziyarah on his behalf, since he was under the watchful eyes of the ruling Abbasid establishment.[39]

Despite the above, some have raised a point claiming the words of Imam Askari refer to the visitation of forty believers, not the visitation of Imam Hussain's shrine during Arbaeen.[40]

In response, this claim seems unsubstantiated and unsupported with evidence. Several questions regarding this interpretation must be answered. Why would 40 believers need to be visited? Does this mean 40 Shias only? When should this visitation take place? Across a year or throughout one's lifespan? Why do we not have other similar commands from the Ahlulbayt ؑ? What characteristics should be displayed by these 40 individuals? Should they be in a geographical location or around the world? What are the particulars of this visitation?

B. The narration of Safwan Al-Jammal

Allamah Majlisi has narrated the Ziyarah of Arbaeen from Imam Sadiq ؑ. This is recited by millions of people annually during Arbaeen.[41] The Ziyarah, explained in Chapter 13, outlines the recommendation that Imam Sadiq ؑ presents for the Shia to undertake the visitation at this time.

The practice of the legislators (*Seerat Al-Mutashari'a*)

One way that jurists assess the validity of an act or deed is by studying the lives of those who lived with the Ahlulbayt ؑ, in an attempt to analyse their conduct. They conclude that what they do is dictated by their understanding of instructions from the Ahlulbayt ؑ. This is based

---

[37] 10th Caliph of the Abbasid Caliphate, d.861
[38] Tarikh Al-Tabari, vol.9, p. 185
[39] Marqad Imam Al-Hussain, p.82
[40] Sayid Muqarram, who is an author of a famous Maqtal book, dismissed this claim (p.366) in his book.
[41] Bihar Al-Anwar, vol.98, p.231

on the concept[42] of those who were considered worthy of being companions of the glorious household. It is noticeable that, for centuries, the followers of Ahlulbayt have endeavoured to establish the Ziyarah of Arbaeen, and this has been supported by our scholars. Despite the oppression and difficulties facing the *zuwwar*, the visitation continued, with people giving their lives in the effort to uphold this sign of Allah (*sha'eera*).

The recommendation to visit Imam Hussain every month

The Imams encouraged their followers to visit the grave of Imam Hussain at all times, and certainly at least once a month.

Daoud ibn Farqad narrates:

'I asked Imam Al-Sadiq: 'What is the reward of the one who visits Imam Hussain every month?' Imam replied:

'They will attain the reward of 100,000 martyrs, like that of the battle of Badr.'[43]

The words and action of the Ulema on Ziyarat Arbaeen

Many jurists, theologians, and historians have highlighted and recommended the importance of Ziyarat Arbaeen throughout the centuries. Amongst them include:

- Sheikh Al-Tusi, in his Misbah, who writes:

'The family of Imam Hussain returned from Syria on this day (Arbaeen). Jabir ibn Abdullah Al-Ansari, the companion of the Prophet, reached Karbala from Medina to visit the grave of Imam Hussain. He was the first to perform this visitation. It is recommended to visit the Imam on this day, and this is Ziyarat of Arbaeen.'[44]

---

[42] This is based on the Islamic fiqh principle known as *Seerat Al-Uqala*. This is where the lives and deeds of those close to the Ahlulbayt are examined and used to deduce rulings.
[43] Tahdhib Al-Ahkam, vol.6, p.47
[44] Misbah Al-Mutahajid, p.730

- In his book *'Al-Mazar'*, Sheikh Al-Mufid dedicated a section on the merits of the Arbaeen Ziyarat.[45]

- Allamah Al-Hilli, in his work *'Muntaha Al-Matlab'* says:

'It is recommended to perform his Ziyarah on the day of Arbaeen, which is 20th Safar.'[46]

- Allamah Majlisi, in his Bihar Al-Anwar, comments:

'The virtue of his visitation on the Day of Ashura...as well as the virtue of the Arbaeen Ziyarah...'[47]

- Sheikh Abbas Al-Qummi, the author of Mafatih Jinan, says:

'The day of 20th Safar is the Arbaeen Day. On the opinion of the two sheikhs it is the day the family of Imam Hussain arrived in Karbala...it is recommended to perform the Ziyarah (of the Imam on that day) ...'[48]

Not only did these scholars and more highlight the importance of the Arbaeen visitation, but as discussed in chapter 5, many scholars performed the walk, setting a good example for others to emulate.

---

[45] Al-Mazar, p.53
[46] Muntaha Al-Matlab, vol.2, p.892
[47] Bihar Al-Anwar, vol.98, p.102
[48] Mafatih Al-Jinan, p.395

Chapter 4:

The Historical Significance of the 20th of Safar

One common belief regarding the significance of Arbaeen is the historical date of the return of the captives from Sham towards Karbala, when they visited the graves of the fallen martyrs. Before discussing the details behind the historical basis and different opinions in this regard, it is important to establish a distinction between the actual historical occurrence and the significance of the Arbaeen visitation.

In determining the *Sharia* rulings on a matter and verifying it as obligatory, recommended, permissible, not recommended, or prohibited, the jurists consider several factors. A mere historical reference or occurrence with no supporting evidence from the sources of legislation - namely Qur'an and Sunna - may not be sufficient to conclude a ruling. Crucially, there should be a differentiation between the details of an incident and whether certain actions should take place on that day according to Islamic law.

This is significant when discussing Arbaeen. Scholars have argued that the discussion on whether the Ahlulbayt ﷺ or some companions of the Prophet arrived in Karbala on the 20th of Safar has no bearing on the importance of Ziyarah of Arbaeen. They are two distinctly separate issues. The reason is the undeniable evidence supporting the visitation of Imam Hussain, generally, at all times and, specifically, during Arbaeen. Whether we can prove the Ahlulbayt and the captives arrived in Karbala on this day would not impact the commemoration of Arbaeen. Unfortunately, some have raised misconceptions regarding this, confusing historical and jurisprudential aspects. They present arguments that dismiss the arrival of the caravan of the Ahlulbayt ﷺ in Karbala in Arbaeen and subsequently question whether Arbaeen should be commemorated at all! This reflects a lack of understanding, or possible manipulation of minds, regarding the deduction of Islamic law by scholars. The various historical interpretations regarding the event of the 20th Safar do not affect whether Arbaeen should be upheld.

The Return of the Captives to Karbala

Historical narrations clearly describe how alongside Imam Hussain, most of his male family members as well as companions were slayed on Ashura, his family were taken as captive and paraded across cities. They were first taken to Kufa, Iraq, then forced to travel towards Sham, Syria. The journey also included a number of stops at various towns and villages. After several encounters with Yazid in Damascus, the family were eventually allowed to leave to return to Medina. On their way back, many narrations point to their request to stop in Karbala, to pay their respects to the fallen martyrs, as well as join the decapitated head to the bodies in the graves.

Scholars from within the two major Muslim Schools (Sunni and Shia) have presented a number of opinions on the event of the return of the captives from Syria to Karbala. The main ones are as follows:

1. They arrived in Karbala exactly 40 days after Ashura, having been taken captive from Kufa and Syria. In Karbala, they met Jabir ibn Abdullah Al-Ansari, the noble companion of the Prophet, who had arrived earlier.

2. They spent nearly a year in Damascus and arrived in Karbala on 20th Safar 62AH. It is argued that it would be difficult to travel the whole distance from Karbala to Sham and back within 40 days

3. Only Jabir ibn Abdullah visited the grave of Imam Hussain ؏ on the 20th of Safar 61AH and not the Ahlulbayt. Some argue they returned to Medina from Syria without stopping in Karbala at all.

4. The Caravan of Ahlulbayt visited the graves of the martyrs in Karbala on their return, but not on 20th Safar. Some argue that, due to the slow movement of the camels and other factors, it would not have been possible to cover the distance within 40 days.

5. A few less accepted opinions also exist, such as the Caravan visiting Karbala after leaving Kufa when it was on its way to Syria.

The first and second opinions are most commonly put forward by scholars. From my research and the discussions held with various scholars, especially those in Najaf and Karbala, the most accepted historical opinion is the first one - that the caravan of the Ahlulbayt visited the blessed graves of the martyrs in Karbala forty days after Ashura, in the same year (61AH), upon their return from Syria.

Several prominent scholars have presented their evidence in this regard. One of them is Ayatollah Mohammad Sadiq Al-Sadr. In his lengthy discussion on this matter, he argues the distance between Karbala and Sham is approximately 2000 km, and it is a fact well-known that horses and camels used at that time could cover it within a short period.

Sayid Al-Sadr supports his opinion by citing the jurisprudential ruling regarding the shortening of prayer whilst travelling. Ulema have demonstrated that prayers become shortened (*qasr*) after approximately 43km from the border of the hometown. The reason for this is because it takes a loaded camel one day (from sunrise to sunset) to cover this distance. If the camel has a lesser load, or is carrying a human, it is conceivable that they would cover considerably more than this, especially if they travel at night.

Hence, if we suppose the camel covers 100Km a day, the caravan of the captives would have covered the distance over 20 days. Ayatollah Sadr argues that, if they cover 150km a day over 24 hours (since the above only considers sunset to sunrise), they would have covered the entire distance back and forth in 25 days, leaving 15 days for their stay in Kufa and Sham. He believes no evidence exists that they stayed more than 15 days in both cities.

It is claimed the captives could not stay long periods during the journey to Damascus and were hurried continuously by Yazid's men. This is because of the fear of reprisals and uprisings by the people they met. Also, the return from Sham to Karbala was probably covered much quicker, since they did not stop at many places. This was because the captives were eager to return home and visit the blessed graves in Karbala.[49]

---

[49] Al-Arbaeen wa falsafatul Mashee ila Al-Imam Hussain, p. 46-49

Other scholars have presented the following as evidence supporting the opinion that Arbaeen was forty days after Ashura (ie in the year 61AH):

1. Sayid Mohsin Al-Amin ؒ in his book *A'yaan Al-Shia* points to the Bedouins of Sulayb (living outside Damascus) reaching Iraq from their land in 8 days.
2. The person taking the letter from Yazid to his governor, Ibn Ziyad, in Kufa to release Al-Mukhtar Al-Thaqafi from prison reached Kufa 11 days after leaving Damascus.
3. Mua'wiya died on the 15th of Rajab 60AH, and the news reached Medina within 10 days, since Imam Hussain ؑ left Medina on the 28th Rajab, i.e. 13 days after Mu'wiya's death.
4. One of the established and well-known Muslim Scholars during the medieval era, Abu Rayhan Al-Biruni, was well-versed in physics, mathematics, geography, and astronomy amongst many other sciences. In his book *'Al-Athar Al-Baqiya'*, he states the captives left Kufa towards Damascus on 15th or 20th Muharram, taking 10 or 15 days to reach Sham. The same time for their return to Karbala is not far-fetched, according to this scholar.
5. Historians have documented the Abbasid Caliph Harun with individuals such as Abu Hanifa used to witness the crescent of the month of Dhul Hijja in Baghdad before leaving for the Hajj pilgrimage. This would mean they would take eight days to cover the distance of approximately 1400 km (as they needed to be in Mecca by 7th or 8th of the month).

Based on the above, it is conceivable that one can roughly place a timeline for the movement of the captives towards Kufa, Sham, and back to Karbala. One possibility is as follows:

11th Muharram: The captives are taken to Kufa and arrive there.
16th-18th Muharram: The captives are taken towards Damascus.
29th Muharram-1st Safar: They reach and enter Damascus.
8th-10th Safar: They leave Damascus and head towards Karbala.
20th Safar: They reach Karbala.

While many scholars and historians from within the Shia school have adapted this belief, one cannot entirely dismiss or disrespect the opinion espoused by others that the visitation of Arbaeen by the holy family took place a year later. Irrespective of the opinions, nothing can affect or take away the blessed nature and the significance of the annual multi-million people walk to the City of Martyrs.

What happened on the Day of Arbaeen (20th Safar 61AH) in Karbala?

It is generally accepted that the first person to perform the Ziyarah of the grave of Imam Hussain ﷺ in Karbala was the famous companion of the Prophet Mohammad ﷺ, Jabir ibn Abdullah Al-Ansari. Jabir was a trusted *sahabi*, who lived to meet the 5th Imam of the Ahlulbayt, Imam Mohammad Al-Baqir ﷺ. He was accompanied by his servant, Atiya, and the exact date of when he reached Karbala is unknown. He was blind at that time. Upon his arrival in Karbala, he performed *ghusl* (washing of body) and asked to be taken to the grave of Imam Hussain ﷺ.

'Jabir ibn Abdullah al-Ansari stood at the grave and burst in tears then thrice called out Hussain's name, then he said, "Why a loved one does not answer one who loves him?" But soon, he answered his own query by saying, "How can he answer while his cheeks are torn, his head separated from his body? Yet I bear witness that you are the son of the Seal of Prophets ﷺ, the son of the Master of the Faithful ﷺ, the son of the inseparable ally of piety, the descendant of guidance, the fifth of the fellows of the *kisa*, the son of the master of *naqibs*, the one who was brought up in the lap of the pious, that you were raised on the milk of iman, that you were weaned with Islam, so you were good when you were alive, and you are so when dead. But the hearts of the faithful are not pleased with parting with you, nor do they have any doubt about goodness being yours. So peace of Allah be upon you and His Pleasure. And I bear witness that you treaded the same path treaded before you by your brother [prophet] Zachariyya."

Having said so, Jabir turned his head around the grave as he said, "Assalamo Alaikum, O souls that abide at Hussain's courtyard! I bear witness that you upheld the prayers and paid zakat, enjoined what is right and prohibited what is wrong, struggled against the atheists and adored Allah till death overtook you. By the One Who sent Mohammad, peace of Allah be upon him and upon his Progeny, as His Prophet with the truth, we have a share in what you have earned."

Atiya al-Awfi [his companion leading him, since he was a blind old man] asked him, "How so when we did not descend a valley nor ascend a mountain, nor did we strike with a sword, whereas the heads of these people have been severed from their bodies, their sons have been orphaned and their wives widowed?" Jabir answered: "I heard the Messenger of Allah, whom I very much love, saying, `One who loves a [certain] people will be lodged with them, and one who loves what some people do will have a share in [the rewards of] their deeds.' By the One Who sent Mohammad as a Prophet with the truth, my intention and that of my companions is identical to the one for which Hussain and his companions were all killed."[50]

Sayid Ibn Tawus, in his book *'Al-Luhuf fe Qatla Al-Tufuf'* sheds light on the meeting that took place between Jabir and the arriving caravan of the Ahlulbayt:

'When the women of Hussain left Damascus they asked to be taken to Karbala. Upon reaching there they found Jabir ibn Abdullah Al-Ansari with a few others from Bani Hashem and the family of the Prophet. The latter had come to visit the grave of Imam Hussain. They met them and began to weep, lament and beat their chests. They remained like this for several days.'[51]

One can only imagine the pain and anguish the Ahlulbayt endured when they visited the graves. Undoubtedly, they would remember the tragedy and what befell their own relatives. It is also recorded in history that the heads of the martyrs, which had been paraded to Kufa and Sham, were now joined with their bodies on the Day of Arbaeen. This included the blessed head of Imam Hussain.

---

[50] Maqtal Al-Hussain, p.301-02
[51] Al-Luhuf fe Qatla Al-Tufuf, vol.1, p.114

Chapter 5:

The Benefit of the Arbaeen Walk

There is an agreement amongst many that humans are driven towards tasks and deeds by the extent of benefit attained and harm avoided. Whether it's seeking education, gaining popularity, or seeking a livelihood through employment, there is an underlying outcome expected and shared across these processes: tangible benefits utilised by human beings. Perhaps, the greater the reward, the more we enthusiastically approach these 'tasks'. For example, many people would struggle with the notion of working in a company or an institution for years, without receiving any remuneration or financial reward.

The ultimate wisdom of the Almighty ﷻ is such that, as the Creator, He knows fully well what drives us to perform tasks and deeds. Hence, we find the Holy Qur'an pointing to the benefits of certain acts of worship, even though believers are instructed to trust God and submit in their willingness to worship Him.

As an example, the daily prayers are prescribed for Muslims, so they continuously remember God and stay connected with the Divine:

إِنَّنِي أَنَا اللَّهُ لَا إِلَهَ إِلَّا أَنَا فَاعْبُدْنِي وَأَقِمِ الصَّلَاةَ لِذِكْرِي

'Indeed I am Allah — there is no god except Me. So, worship Me, and maintain the prayer for My remembrance.'[52]

Yet, the Qur'an points to an important realisation: Performing prayers is crucial in the soul's defence mechanism against vice and evil. Adherence to Salah and its correct maintenance strengthens the ability to repel sins and transgressions throughout our lives:

---

[52] Holy Qur'an (20:14)

اتْلُ مَا أُوحِيَ إِلَيْكَ مِنَ الْكِتَابِ وَأَقِمِ الصَّلَاةَ ۖ إِنَّ الصَّلَاةَ تَنْهَىٰ عَنِ الْفَحْشَاءِ وَالْمُنْكَرِ

'Recite what has been revealed to you of the Book, and maintain the prayer. Indeed, the prayer prevents indecencies and wrongs...'[53]

The Qur'an is categorically emphasising that not only are prayers a beautiful form of *dhikr* (remembrance of Allah) as they enhance the spiritual experience and solidify the connection with our creator, but they also have the incredible power to bring about social harmony within society. Interactions between people are strengthened when believers utilise the power of prayers to reflect good ethical traits when dealing and interacting with others. Hence, scholars emphasise that an important sign of the acceptance of *Salah* is whether it has had a positive impact on the social etiquette of its performer and has prevented wrongful practice.

What is important is that, not only are we promised eternal reward in God's pleasure in the hereafter, but submitting to His will also brings about positive benefits in our worldly lives.

Another demonstration of this is the annual pilgrimage, known as the Hajj. Despite being obligatory for a Muslim only once in a lifetime, the Qur'an affirms the believers who conduct it appropriately, in accordance with God's laws, will witness several benefits:

وَأَذِّن فِي النَّاسِ بِالْحَجِّ يَأْتُوكَ رِجَالًا وَعَلَىٰ كُلِّ ضَامِرٍ يَأْتِينَ مِن كُلِّ فَجٍّ عَمِيقٍ

'And proclaim the hajj to people: they shall come to you on foot and on lean camels coming from distant places, that they may witness the benefits for them...'[54]

These benefits include spiritual, social, economic, political, and personal gains. The better the act of worship, the more of these are received and felt by the believers. Undoubtedly, this increases the enthusiasm and commitment in approaching these acts of worship.

For centuries, Muslims have endeavoured to build and visit shrines and mausoleums of holy personalities across the world. Many see this as a display of loyalty and love towards these individuals, who have usually left a lasting legacy in the hearts of people. Not surprisingly, such practice

---

[53] Holy Qur'an (29:45)
[54] Holy Qur'an (22:27)

is not confined to the Shia, but rather to most Muslims in various countries. From the Imam Hussain shrine in Cairo, visited by millions annually, to the shrine of Abu Hanifa in Baghdad, the belief in Ziyarah (holy visitation) has been integral within the teachings of most Muslims, including the Sunni denomination. In my travels to Turkey and Egypt, I visited these holy sites and witnessed first-hand the devotion and love expressed towards the people buried there.

The Arbaeen Ziyarah is one of the greatest manifestations of this love towards the holy family of the Prophet ﷺ. The millions who undertake the walk from various parts of Iraq towards the city of Karbala include people of many nationalities, but also individuals from various non-Shia Muslim denominations. In addition, people of other faiths have participated in the walk, as documented by officials. Despite the incredible dedication displayed by those serving the visitors of Imam Hussain ؏ and the grand demonstration of love towards the grandson of the Prophet by the millions visiting, many witness a wide variety of benefits in undertaking this act of worship. These include personal, social, economic, and political gains.

The Personal Benefits

This is related to advantages that can be attained for the personal progression of the visitor, sometimes witnessed after the walk and upon return to their homelands. Importantly, some of these gains are obtained if the visitor is seeking self-development and wants to utilise this life-changing experience for their benefit.

A. Patience and solitude

An important dimension of the acts of worship designated in Islamic teachings is the goal of enhancing *sabr*, or patience, which would ultimately help the human being in countering the many challenges presented to them in life. Patience is a wonderful virtue, needed to achieve success in this world and the Hereafter. It is a trait emphasised in the Qur'an and the teachings of the Ahlulbayt ؏:

وَبَشِّرِ الصَّابِرِينَ

'...and give good news to the patient.'[55]

إِنَّ اللَّهَ مَعَ الصَّابِرِينَ

'...indeed Allah is with the patient.'[56]

إِنَّمَا يُوَفَّى الصَّابِرُونَ أَجْرَهُم بِغَيْرِ حِسَابٍ

'...Indeed the patient will be paid in full their reward without any reckoning.'[57]

The importance of inculcating patience within our conduct is mentioned in numerous narrations, such as one in particular from Imam Ali ؏:

'The similitude of patience to faith is that of the head to the body; if it separated the body has no use. Likewise, if there is no patience, there is no faith.'[58]

During the Arbaeen walk, the visitors typically undertake a journey that involves walking for tens of kilometres. They usually encounter congestion, uncomfortable sleep, threat of terrorism, unconventional sanitation (especially for those from the West not used to traditional Middle Eastern bathrooms), and extremes of weather. I have witnessed some *zuwwar* who walk despite pain in their bodies or legs or other forms of physical illness due to the strenuous nature of the journey. In addition, they may face behaviours from a small number that might irritate or anger them, including pushing to attain food. In many instances, the visitors sleep with tens of others within a tent or a large hall, encountering frequent sleep disturbances caused by noise such as snoring or people talking, or a lack of space.

These and more are just some challenges faced in this endeavour, yet they exist for specific reasons. Like the Hajj pilgrimage, the visitor encountering this would need to have the mental and physical strength to

---

[55] Holy Qur'an (2:155)
[56] Holy Qur'an (2:153)
[57] Holy Qur'an (39:10)
[58] Al-Amthal, vol.7, p.393

embrace these difficulties. Ultimately, the demonstration of patience across the walk will equip the believers to stand up to the tribulations of life with patience and strength, appreciating the universal law of trials that applies to all and is present to make us better human beings.

It is also the case that people have different thresholds of patience, in terms of their capability to deal with that which they face. Experiencing the Arbaeen walk with the correct mind-set can surely raise this threshold, enabling us to seek the patience we so desperately need to be amongst the righteous.

One can admire the strength of the Ahlulbayt ﷺ, including the caravan of captives, who had to endure a much more difficult journey, whilst feeling the whips and sticks of the enemy. They passed from one city to another, whilst bearing humiliation and torture, yet remaining resolute and firm in faith. Hence we read in the Ziyarah:

"...the angels are surprised by your patience..."[59]

B. Release of tensions and stress

Due to the increasing work-load and pressures of life, many of us frequently encounter feelings of stress, tension, or anxiety. These can be detrimental to health, wellbeing, spirituality, and self-progression.

While walking towards the land of Karbala, the visitors of Imam Hussain ﷺ lose themselves in the sea of the devotees, and the everyday stresses of life seem to disappear as they walk towards the man whose faith and strength never cease to amaze. Many are absorbed by the atmosphere, which is generally characterised by people who have an awe-inspiring willingness to serve others and be of as much help as they can. The air is heavy with the melancholy sounds of grief and sorrow. The raw sadness felt across the walk only affirms the connection the believer seeks to establish with the Master of Martyrs, whilst reflecting on how, through tragedy, the movement of Imam Hussain remains eternally influential.

The visitor will listen to *latmiyyas* (eulogies) and beat their chest, meet others less fortunate, seek to serve other *zuwwar*, chant *'Labbayk Ya Hussain'*, and capture mental images that will inspire them forever.

---

[59] Ziyarat Al-Nahiya Al-Muqadassa, Mafatihul Jinan, p.234

It is also worth noting, throughout the many years I have been honoured to undertake this spiritual journey, making phone calls or connecting to the internet is usually very difficult. Perhaps advantageously, this allows for a better focus on the experience and minimises distractions throughout the walk.

When speaking to many *zuwwar* who have undertaken this journey from various parts of the world, the clear majority seek to return to perform the walk to Karbala. The numbers participating has increased annually. This highlights that, despite the difficulties and challenges, the *zuwwar* witness many benefits and recognize the importance this walk plays in their lives.

C. Attaining health benefits

For centuries, scientific research has demonstrated the numerous benefits, both physical and mental, of walking. From a report entitled 'The benefits of regular walking for health, well-being and the environment' published by a think tank in 2012, the following conclusion is derived:

'Walking is one of the least expensive and most broadly accessible forms of physical activity. It is rarely associated with physical injury and can easily be adopted by people of all ages, including those who have never participated in physical activity. Studies have shown that walking has higher levels of adherence than other forms of physical activity, possibly because it is convenient and overcomes many of the commonly perceived barriers to physical activity: lack of time, lack of fitness or lack of skill.'[60]

The report also indicated that regular walking improves balance, halves the risk of Alzheimer's disease over five years, engages abdominal muscles, and improves heart health by increasing heart rate and circulation. Many more benefits have been detailed by scientific findings. This is especially the case if the walk is sustained over time.

Interestingly, this is also supported in Islamic teachings. Jabir narrates that a group of people complained of tiredness to Prophet Mohammad ﷺ. He prayed for them and told them to walk at pace. Upon trying this, they reported their condition improved.[61]

---

[60] C3 collaborating for Health, September 2012
[61] Majma' Al-Zawa'id, vol.5, p.276

D. Reflection and introspection

Due to the increasing trend of being busy, either with gadgets or through other means, we may find it difficult in our daily lives to set aside time for ourselves and engage in healthy contemplation. The practice of *tafakkur*, known as pondering and reflection, has been emphasised in the Qur'an on numerous occasions:

الَّذِينَ يَذْكُرُونَ اللَّهَ قِيَامًا وَقُعُودًا وَعَلَىٰ جُنُوبِهِم وَيَتَفَكَّرُونَ فِي خَلْقِ السَّمَاوَاتِ وَالْأَرْضِ رَبَّنَا مَا خَلَقْتَ هَٰذَا بَاطِلًا سُبْحَانَكَ فَقِنَا عَذَابَ النَّارِ

'Those who remember Allah standing, sitting, and lying on their sides, and reflect on the creation of the heavens and the earth [and say], 'Our Lord, You have not created this in vain! Immaculate are You! Save us from the punishment of the Fire'.[62]

Such contemplation allows us to consolidate our thoughts, focus on objectives, and reaffirm our commitment towards the goal of our existence: seeking the pleasure of the Almighty ﷻ. Whilst we might be very busy back home, attempting to find the time and space to undertake this act of worship, the walk to Karbala is a crucial opportunity to engage in introspection and self-accountability. Questions that the visitor should seek to think about include:

How have I lived my life, so far?
How can I be inspired by Ashura to improve my spiritual progression?
How can I contribute positively and improve the lives of others?
How do I ensure my family is adherent to the path of truth?
How do I protect myself from satanic thoughts and temptations?

These and many more questions can be uniquely tailored around one's individual preferences. At the same time, the walk enables us to reignite our passion towards serving humanity through the Qur'an and Ahlulbayt ﷺ. Through a positive mind-set and a determined attitude, the visitor of Imam Hussain will seek to strengthen their willpower and self-

---

[62] Holy Qur'an (3:191)

control via their quest for virtue and righteousness. Similarly, reflection should also be infused with the remembrance of God, expressing gratitude for the unquantifiable bounties bestowed upon us, especially the opportunity to be part of the biggest annual peaceful gathering in the world.

E. Enhancing spirituality

The most outstanding characteristic in the life of Imam Hussain ؏, the Ahlulbayt, and the Prophets is their association with God and their absolute submission to Him. A visitor to Karbala, through the effort of walking for tens of kilometres, would seek their heart to be illuminated with guidance and would yearn to taste the sweetness of proximity to God. Throughout the journey, many visitors stop to perform congregational prayers on time at *mawkibs* and *hussayniyas*. This happens across a few days. The establishment of congregational prayers on such a scale continuously may not be something many have performed before.

Not only does this and other collective acts of worship, such as reciting Ziyarah or attending majalis, bring them reward from Allah ﷻ, but it can also set the scene for further practice upon returning to their homelands. For many it sets a new beginning and a fresh start towards practicing faith and adhering to Allah's commands.

Additionally, the spirit of generosity and serving others can only inspire millions to do what they can in the name of Imam Hussain ؏. According to narrations, the closest position attained by humans to their Creator is when they place happiness in the hearts of other believers. It is envisaged that, collectively, the visitors can motivate each other to utilise the experience of Arbaeen in re-examining their relationship with Allah ﷻ by looking at ways to strengthen the bond and purify the heart.

The spirit of giving for the sake of Allah includes the rejection of egoism and self-love. These vices and others, such as arrogance and prejudice, are impediments towards a submissive heart to the Almighty ﷻ. Throughout the various stages of this journey, the incredible degree of service, support, and assistance displayed by those who want to make the *zuwwar* happy should deter evil thoughts of jealousy and satanic tendencies towards self-glorification. The more determined and focused we are, the greater the outcomes after the journey is over.

The Social Benefits of the Arbaeen walk

A. Brotherhood and unity

Across many centuries, human beings have suffered extensively, with the politics of division, hatred, bigotry, discrimination, and prejudice. Millions of innocent souls have been killed due to racist tendencies, whilst many have been displaced from their lands because of ethnic cleansing. Islam denounces racism and discrimination, encouraging its followers to display love, respect, coexistence, and a strong sense of brotherhood. Diversity in creation is one of the hallmarks of the wisdom of the Almighty ﷻ, and He informs mankind they must embrace this to get to know each other:

يا أَيُّهَا النَّاسُ إِنَّا خَلَقْنَاكُم مِن ذَكَرٍ وَأُنثَىٰ وَجَعَلْنَاكُمْ شُعُوبًا وَقَبَائِلَ لِتَعَارَفُوا ۚ إِنَّ أَكْرَمَكُمْ عِندَ اللَّهِ أَتْقَاكُمْ ۚ إِنَّ اللَّهَ عَلِيمٌ خَبِيرٌ

'O mankind! Indeed, We created you from a male and a female, and made you nations and tribes that you may identify yourselves with one another. Indeed, the noblest of you in the sight of Allah is the most God wary among you. Indeed, Allah is all-knowing, all-aware.'[63]

In his famous instructions to his newly appointed governor of Egypt, Malik Al-Ashtar, Imam Ali ؑ famously established the foundation of a believer's interaction with others:

'People are of two kinds: either your brother in faith or equal in humanity.'[64]

In modern times, certain groups, politicians, parts of the media, and other extreme-minded individuals have attempted to espouse hatred, division, disunity, and discrimination. This has invariably given rise to victimization and harassment of many, especially Muslims. The Shia have been victims of hatred and violence for hundreds of years.

One of the beautiful outcomes of the Arbaeen walk, completed by millions annually, is the enhancement of the spirit of brotherhood and social cohesion. I have witnessed people from various countries,

---

[63] Holy Qur'an (49:13)
[64] Nahjul Balagha, Letter 53

including Thailand, China, Brazil, Ghana and Mozambique participating with love in their hearts and loyalty on their lips. What unites them is the love of Imam Hussain ﷺ, and this is expressed through service to each other. Whether it's food, accommodation, foot massages, washing clothes, warm drinks, or medicines, people are not characterised according to their background or ethnicity. The sense of unity can be felt across the walk and beyond, and their unquestionable love for the beloved grandson of the Holy Prophet provides adrenalin in abundance.

The constant encouragement, prayers, and words of support on the path to Karbala indicates the real sense of brotherhood amongst the visitors. Due to the constant threat of extremist elements attempting to infiltrate and cause widespread carnage, people are constantly on the lookout for each other, alert to spot any potential dangers.

Wonderful sights are beheld such as people helping and encouraging the elderly and disabled, others embracing young children as they walk whilst some share necessities such as blankets and medicine. These send a powerful and unrelenting message of unison and harmony.

Whether they are rich or poor, men or women, young or old, people of power or not, the educated and the not, they walk side by side, knowing such diversity was a hallmark of the army of Imam Hussain ﷺ, and that superiority in the eyes of Allah ﷻ is only measured by God-consciousness.

Stopping by at *mawkibs*, people often initiate conversations with their fellow *za'ir* (visitor). Many establish bonds of friendship and seek to alleviate each other's hardships and difficulties.

Undoubtedly, such social unity brings happiness to the heart of the awaited saviour Imam Mehdi ﷺ, who, with the rest of the Ahlulbayt, taught brotherly love and care.

Imam Sadiq ﷺ is reported to have said:

'A believer is a brother of another believer, like one body. If one of the parts is in pain, the rest of the body feels the suffering...'[65]

---

[65] Al-Kafi, vol.2, p.166

B. Reinforcing the Identity

Whilst walking alongside the thousands on the road to Karbala, the visitor feels an immense sense of pride and honour to be considered a follower of the Ahlulbayt ﷺ. At a time when some are feeling the full force of Islamophobia and 'Shiaphobia', this sense of belonging and the unified identity of the followers of Imam Hussain ﷺ rejuvenates their spirit and increases self-assurance. The freedom to practice and mourn, coupled with the atmosphere of grief in remembering the tragedy of Ashura, evokes much emotion, usually leading to a stronger connection with these holy individuals.

Imam Ali is reported to have said:

> *'Our Shia display happiness when we are happy and are grieving when we grieve...'*[66]

Participation in the Arbaeen walk also gives confidence to the believers living in the West to be ambassadors of this act of devotion in their countries. When speaking with others, who may not have heard of the millions who walk, the description of the experience gives rise to a better profile and reputation for Shia Muslims around the world.

C. Social Support

Despite estimations suggesting there are between 10 to 20 million visitors each Arbaeen, the supply of food, water, and essential necessities has not been adversely affected nor diminished. *Mawkibs* eagerly invite the *zuwwar* to eat or take rest, making it their pride to serve them with anything. Although some have attempted to calculate the cost of providing food to such a sheer volume of people, it will undoubtedly be in the millions of dollars. The majority of the money spent is via donation or from the *mawkibs* gathering funds throughout the year.

The support presented to the needy, homeless, and the orphans throughout the walk is also very evident. Several leading organizations, dedicated to alleviating the suffering of the poor and the destitute, set up desks and *mawkibs* inviting donations. The visitor of Imam Hussain ﷺ is

---

[66] Bihar Al-Anwar, vol.10, p.114

reminded that meaningful participation in the walk should be concluded by committing to positively changing the lives of others as much as possible. By sponsoring one of the estimated 4 million orphans in Iraq, the visitor is putting in practice an important lesson from the illustrious life of the Imam ﷺ.

I also witnessed, throughout the years, the willingness of some brothers and sisters to donate generously towards the *mawkibs* and those offering services to the visitors. Similarly, some have approached the needy and aided them in whatever way possible.

The opportunity to make this positive contribution is presented by being in this place and walking alongside the other *zuwwar*. Due to absent-mindedness or a busy schedule, we may sometimes overlook the pressing requirements of others and need to be reminded about them continuously. Walking to Karbala is a great way to increase exposure and highlight the ever-growing needs of those less fortunate.

D. Solidarity with the Martyrs

Plagued with wars and acts of terror, the Iraqi people have experienced years of hardship and the devastating loss of innocent life. In defending the holy shrines and their country, thousands have given up their lives participating in combat against extremist groups, such as Daesh (ISIS) and Al-Qaeda. Throughout the walk, their images are plastered in many places, reminding the visitors of their dedication in giving their lives in the path of Imam Hussain ﷺ. At the same time, one can identify that many of these martyrs were young men responding to the call of the *Marjiyya* without hesitation.[67]

Participating in the walk allows the visitor to appreciate the sacrifice offered by these selfless heroes and how they are defenders of humanity against the evil of terrorism. Realisation dawns that, without the wisdom of our ulema and the bravery of our brothers and the support of their families, the Arbaeen walk might not have been possible. The *zuwwar* are reminded of the need to pray for those who continue to fight at the battlefields, as well as the importance of supporting their families especially the widows and orphans as well as others as much as one can.

---

[67] In June 2015, Ayatollah Sistani issued a famous edict calling Iraqis to take part in armed resistance against the advancing Daesh terrorists.

E. Expression of strength against the enemies

Videos and images of the millions marching peacefully to Karbala from different cities in Iraq through the month of Safar are powerful depictions of strength and unity against the enemies of Islam. Despite the various targeting of the Shia in many countries through suicide bombings, assassinations, imprisonments, or banning of publications, the walk of Arbaeen demonstrates the Shia Muslims will not compromise their faith nor will they be defeated. This is also a demonstration of the powerful legacy of Imam Hussain ؑ and his influence upon the masses. Despite the near 1400-year gap between the event of Ashura, the millions of men and women, young or old, are not fazed by the threat of terrorism and other challenges. They emerge with conviction and passion to recall the sacrifice of the Ahlulbayt ؑ. This is exactly what the brave and eloquent sister of Imam Hussain, Sayida Zainab ؑ, famously uttered in the courtyard of the tyrant Umayyad Yazid:

'You may contrive and try however much you can. By Him who honoured us with revelation, the Book and Prophethood, you cannot achieve our status, nor reach our position, nor can you effect our mention, nor remove from yourself that shame and dishonour that is now your lot because of perpetrating excess and oppression on us. Your word now is weak and your days are counted. Beware of the day when the announcer would announce the curse of Allah on the oppressors and the unjust.'[68]

Chants and banners proclaiming *'Hayhat Minna Al-Thilla'* (Never will we surrender) can be heard and seen across the walk, signifying the determination of people in remaining dignified and never bowing towards tyranny and injustice. This was the call of Imam Hussain ؑ 1400 years ago, and it is being duly carried by generations who have committed to learn from him and to remain faithful in his path.

---

[68] Maqtal Al-Muqarram, p. 299

The theological and religious benefits

A. The establishment of *Wilayah* and *Bara'a* (rejection)

An important part of the branches of faith, as stipulated within Shia Islam, is the acceptance of the full authority and Divinely chosen status of the Holy Prophet Mohammad ﷺ and his Ahlulbayt ﷺ. This concept, known as *wilayah*, is established through numerous Quranic verses and many narrations. For example:

إِنَّما وَلِيُّكُمُ اللَّهُ وَرَسولُهُ وَالَّذينَ آمَنُوا الَّذينَ يُقيمونَ الصَّلاةَ وَيُؤتونَ الزَّكاةَ وَهُم راكِعونَ

'Your guardian is only Allah, His Apostle, and the faithful who maintain the prayer and give the zakāt while bowing down.'[69]

The rejection and distancing from their enemies is important, in line with Quranic direction:

لا تَجِدُ قَومًا يُؤمِنونَ بِاللَّهِ وَاليَومِ الآخِرِ يُوادّونَ مَن حادَّ اللَّهَ وَرَسولَهُ وَلَو كانوا آباءَهُم أَو أَبناءَهُم أَو إِخوانَهُم أَو عَشيرَتَهُم ۚ أُولٰئِكَ كَتَبَ في قُلوبِهِمُ الإيمانَ وَأَيَّدَهُم بِروحٍ مِنهُ

'You will not find a people believing in Allah and the Last Day endearing those who oppose Allah and His Apostle even though they were their own parents, or children, or brothers, or kinsfolk. [For] such, He has written faith into their hearts and strengthened them with a spirit from Him...'[70]

Imam Al-Redha ﷺ is reported to have said:

'The completion of religion is (the belief in) our authority (wilayah) and the rejection of our enemies.'[71]

The visitors to Karbala, walking passionately alongside their brothers and sisters, demonstrate a manifestation of the loyalty and wilayah to the Ahlulbayt ﷺ.

---

[69] Holy Qur'an (5:55)
[70] Holy Qur'an (58:22)
[71] Bihar Al-Anwar, vol.27, p.58

'I am peaceful to those whom you are peaceful to, and stand against those whom you stood against till the Day of Judgement...[72]*'*

By uttering these words in Ziyarah they are proclaiming their loyalty to the Holy household and exhibit unwavering commitment to the Prophet of Islam and his progeny. Practically, this would mean that whatever pleases the glorious household should be performed and whatever displeases them should be avoided. This intense love for Imam Hussain would mean dedication towards all the values he stood for and rejection to that which he sought to uproot.

B. Recognition of the *isma* (error-free grace) of the Imam

The millions walking to Karbala will recite, as far as the Ziyarah of Imam Hussain is concerned, the following:

'I bear witness that verily you were a light in the sublime loins and purified wombs. The impurities of ignorance did not even touch you, nor could its soiled and dirty bearing ever smear you. I bear witness that, verily, you are the mainstay of the religion, and the supporter of the faithful ones. I bear witness that, verily, you are a pious, God-fearing, favourite, wise and rightly guided (Imam). I bear witness that the Imams, in your progeny, are the words of piety. And the signs of guidance and the safe handle of Islam, and the decisive argument for the humankind.'[73]

This testimony is important, since there have been calls throughout history and during recent times questioning the legitimacy of the movement of Imam Hussain . The Umayyad propaganda machine spread the false belief that the Imam did not respect the caliph of the time and therefore deserved to be killed. Sadly, such falsehood continues to be echoed today.[74]

By participating in this huge show of loyalty, the visitor declares that the statements, movement, sacrifice, and stance of Imam Hussain are a part of Allah's commands, and the Imam is error-free (*Ma'soom*). This is established in the holy Qur'an:

---

[72] Mafatihul Jinan, p.279
[73] Mafatihul Jinan, p.399
[74] The Saudi Mufti, Abdul-Aziz Aal-Sheikh declared this on Muharram 2009 on Al-Majd TV

إِنَّمَا يُرِيدُ اللَّهُ لِيُذْهِبَ عَنكُمُ الرِّجْسَ أَهْلَ البَيْتِ وَيُطَهِّرَكُم تَطْهِيرًا

'...verily Allah wants to protect you oh family of the Prophet from impurities and cleanse you a thorough purification.'[75]

C. Pledging allegiance

A study of the events preceding 10th Muharram, especially the sermons delivered by Imam Hussain ﷺ, reveals the extent of his determination to stand against the injustice of Yazid. For example, when the governor of Medina demanded he give allegiance to the Umayyad tyrant, the response was unwavering:

'We are the household of the Prophet, the substance of the Message, the ones visited by the angels; it is through us that Allah initiates and concludes. Yazid is a man of sin, a drunkard, a murderer of the soul the killing of which Allah has prohibited, a man who is openly promiscuous. A man like me shall never swear the oath of allegiance to a man like him.'[76]

Participation in the Arbaeen walk is akin to standing in solidarity with the Imam ﷺ and his revolution against oppression. It is also a stance of defiance against the oppressive rulers and tyrants who terrorise people. Therefore, throughout history, many have attempted to prohibit the walk or Ziyarah, threatening persecution and imprisonment. This includes the likes of the Abbasid ruler Al-Mutawakil, who promised to amputate the hands and legs of those who visit Imam Hussain ﷺ. Similarly, the despotic regime of Saddam Hussain executed thousands caught secretly walking to Karbala throughout the 1980s and 90s. Yet, despite this, it is God's decree that the walk today is the world's largest annual peaceful gathering and is going from strength to strength. The following Quranic verse illustrates this beautifully:

---

[75] Holy Qur'an (33:33)
[76] Maqtal Al-Muqarram, p. 29

يُرِيدُونَ لِيُطْفِئُوا نُورَ اللَّهِ بِأَفْوَاهِهِم وَاللَّهُ مُتِمُّ نُورِهِ وَلَوْ كَرِهَ الْكَافِرُونَ

'They desire to put out the light of Allah with their mouths, but Allah shall perfect His light though the faithless should be averse.'[77]

The calls of 'Ya Hussain' by the visitors reverberate across hundreds of kilometres of the walk to Karbala and are a response to the Imam's call for help on the Day of Ashura, when he famously said: 'Hal min Nasirin Yansura' (Is there anyone to help us?). The message of strength and solidarity with the Imam, coupled with the rejection of tyranny and oppression, is keenly felt and witnessed, trembling the heart of every tyrant and giving hope to those oppressed throughout the world.

D. The demand for the rights

The Arbaeen walk is considered a massive international conference for the followers of the Ahlulbayt. People gather from many parts of the world and display their devotion towards the lantern of guidance and the ship of salvation that is Imam Hussain. One objective is to send a powerful message to the countries with Shia Muslim residents, who have developed policies of discrimination and harassment against them. The message is clear: The Shia are not few, nor do they lack resources or effective leadership. They will not tolerate oppression; nor will they be ignored. They should be treated equally and fairly with other citizens.

Some of those coming from oppressive regimes utilise this opportunity to highlight the extent of tyranny they are facing by holding solidarity programmes, establishing their own *mawkibs*, distributing books and pamphlets, and displaying images of martyrs who gave their lives in defence of human rights and dignity.

---

[77] Holy Qur'an (61:8)

Chapter 6:

The Walk to Karbala: Background and Philosophy

Walking is an important physical movement practiced by human beings and animals. It is a necessity that develops throughout early life and becomes an essential tool to fulfil necessary objectives.

The health benefits of walking have been established and are generally well-known. Regular walking strengthens the heart, lowers blood pressure, prevents dementia, improves the mood, and strengthens muscles. More is mentioned about this in chapter 5 on the benefits of the walk.

Walking in the Qur'an

The extensive nature of Islamic teachings is such that it covers many facets in the life of human beings, including walking. In the Holy Qur'an, Allah ﷻ establishes that walking is a blessing from The Almighty towards His creation:

وَاللَّهُ خَلَقَ كُلَّ دَابَّةٍ مِن مَاءٍ ۖ فَمِنْهُم مَّن يَمْشِي عَلَىٰ بَطْنِهِ وَمِنْهُم مَّن يَمْشِي عَلَىٰ رِجْلَيْنِ وَمِنْهُم مَّن يَمْشِي عَلَىٰ أَرْبَعٍ ۚ يَخْلُقُ اللَّهُ مَا يَشَاءُ ۚ إِنَّ اللَّهَ عَلَىٰ كُلِّ شَيْءٍ قَدِيرٌ

'Allah created every animal from water. Among them are some that creep upon their bellies, and among them are some that walk on two feet, and among them are some that walk on four. Allah creates whatever He wishes. Indeed, Allah has power over all things.'[78]

---

[78] Holy Qur'an (24:45)

Qur'anic verses also discuss the important etiquette regarding walking that should be observed by believers:

A. Humility

وَعِبادُ الرَّحمٰنِ الَّذينَ يَمشونَ عَلَى الأَرضِ هَونًا وَإِذا خاطَبَهُمُ الجاهِلونَ قالوا سَلامًا

'The servants of the All-beneficent are those who walk humbly on the earth, and when the ignorant address them, say, 'Peace!''[79]

B. The direction of life under God's guidance

أَوَمَن كانَ مَيتًا فَأَحيَيناهُ وَجَعَلنا لَهُ نورًا يَمشي بِهِ فِي النّاسِ كَمَن مَثَلُهُ فِي الظُّلُماتِ لَيسَ بِخارِجٍ مِنها

'Is he who was lifeless, then We gave him life and provided him with a light by which he walks among the people, like one who dwells in a manifold darkness which he cannot leave?'[80]

C. Avoiding the walk of the arrogant

وَلا تَمشِ فِي الأَرضِ مَرَحًا ۖ إِنَّكَ لَن تَخرِقَ الأَرضَ وَلَن تَبلُغَ الجِبالَ طولًا

'Do not walk exultantly on the earth. Indeed, you will neither pierce the earth, nor reach the mountains in height.'[81]

D. Measured pace

وَلا تُصَعِّر خَدَّكَ لِلنّاسِ وَلا تَمشِ فِي الأَرضِ مَرَحًا ۖ إِنَّ اللَّهَ لا يُحِبُّ كُلَّ مُختالٍ فَخورٍ

'Do not turn your cheek disdainfully from the people, and do not walk exultantly on the earth. Indeed, Allah does not like any swaggering braggart.'[82]

---

[79] Holy Qur'an (25:63)
[80] Holy Qur'an (6:122)
[81] Holy Qur'an (17:37)
[82] Holy Qur'an (31:18)

E. Modesty in walking

فَجَاءَتْهُ إِحْدَاهُمَا تَمْشِي عَلَى اسْتِحْيَاءٍ

'Then one of the two women approached him, walking modestly.'[83]

Narrations on walking

In Islamic law, walking is classified as permissible, recommended, or prohibited. This is related to the intention and outcome that results from the intentional walk of the human.

Walking is of course permissible Islamically, unless it constitutes walking towards an act of disobedience of God. However, if used to worship Allah ﷻ and fulfil His commands, then it also becomes recommended. This includes walking to visit the ill, performing prayers at a mosque, fulfilling the needs of a believer, or participating in the visitation of holy personalities for example. Narrations from the Ahlulbayt ﷺ have highlighted this:

A. Walking to the Mosque

The Holy Prophet Mohammad ﷺ is narrated to have said:

'Whomsoever walks to a mosque, they will attain, for every step they undertake until their return home, ten good deeds, the removal of ten sins and the raising of ten levels.'[84]

B. Walking towards congregational prayers

The Holy Prophet ﷺ has said:

'Whomsoever walks to a mosque seeking congregational prayers attains, for every step, 1000 good deeds, and is raised likewise. If they die at this state, Allah will make 70,000 angels to look after him in his grave, asking for his forgiveness until he is resurrected.'[85]

---

83 Holy Qur'an (28:25)
84 Wasa'il Al-Shia, vol.5, p.201
85 Tahdhib Al-Ahkam, vol.3, p.255.

C. Walking for the Hajj pilgrimage

Imam Sadiq is narrated to have said:

'Allah has not been worshipped like through (maintaining) silence and walking towards His House.'[86]

This was the practice of the Ahlulbayt . Imam Sadiq has said Imam Hassan walked towards Hajj 23 times in his life.[87]

D. Walking for Umrah

Abdullah ibn Al-Hasan narrates from his grandfather, Ali ibn Ja'far (Al-Sadiq), who said:

'We left with my brother Musa (Al-Kadhim) for Umrah in four occasions. He walked to Makkah in all of them with his family...'[88]

E. Walking in a funeral

Imam Sadiq is narrated to have said:

'Whomsoever takes part in a funeral, performing the prayers then returning, they have reward equivalent to (weight of) the Uhud mountain.'[89]

F. Walking for the fulfilment of needs of believers

Imam Sadiq :

'Whoever walks to fulfil the needs of their believing brothers, seeking the pleasure of Allah, and fulfils their need will receive from the Almighty the reward of an accepted Hajj and umrah, the fasting of two months from the sacred

---

[86] Wasa'il Al-Shia, vol.5, p.201
[87] Wasa'il Al-Shia, vol.11, p.78
[88] Wasa'il Al-Shia, vol.14, p.317
[89] Al-Kafi, vol.3, p.173

months, and I'tikaf[90] during these two months in Masjid Al-Haram (Ka'ba). If they walk with intention of fulfilling the wish but it does not materialize, Allah will grant them reward of an accepted Hajj. Therefore, seek righteousness.'[91]

G. Walking to visit believers

It is narrated that the Prophet Mohammad ﷺ said:

'Whoever walks to visit their brother, they will be granted, for each step, the emancipation of 100,000 slaves, raised 100,000 degrees, and 100,000 sins will be erased.'[92]

H. Walking to reconcile between people

The Messenger of Allah is narrated to have said:

'Whomsoever walks to reconcile between a lady and her husband, Allah will grant them the reward of 1000 martyrs killed truly for the sake of God. For every step they undertake and word they utter (in this), they attain reward of a year's worship, in which the night was spent in ibada(worship) and the day fasting.'[93]

I. Walking to seek Knowledge

The Messenger of Allah said:

'Verily the angels place their wings under the feet of the one who is seeking knowledge.'[94]

As can be seen, many actions performed by walking for the Almighty are considered worthy of praise and reward. The narrations point to the walk before the good deed as the foundation needed towards seeking the pleasure of God.

---

[90] An act of worship in Islam where a believer spends at least 3 days in a mosque fully devoted to God in worship
[91] Al-Kafi, vol.2, p.194 - 195
[92] Wasa'il Al-Shia, vol.14, p.590
[93] Wasa'il Al-Shia, vol. 16, p.344
[94] Lisan Al-Arab, vol.15, p.232

The Excellence of the Walk to Karbala

Several established books of narrations have dedicated sections detailing the merit of the walk towards the blessed shrine of the Master of Martyrs, Imam Hussain ﷺ, in Karbala. This includes Sheikh ibn Qawlaweh in his famous work 'Kamil Al-Ziyarat', such as chapter 49 of his book, entitled 'The merits of visiting Hussain ﷺ on foot or other means of transport…'

Sheikh Al-Hur Al-Amili, in his monumental work, 'Wasa'il Al-Shia', dedicated section 41 to listing some of these narrations. The section is entitled: 'The Merit of the walk for Ziyarah of Hussain ﷺ'. A sample of these narrations is found below:

1. Imam Sadiq ﷺ is reported to have said:

'When a person leaves from their house seeking the visitation of the grave of Hussain ibn Ali ﷺ, every step they undertake will result in a good deed and the wiping of a sin...'[95]

2. Imam Sadiq ﷺ:

'When a man leaves his family to visit the grave of Imam Hussain ﷺ, with the first step he takes, all his sins are forgiven. Then as he travels, he will become further purified. Once he arrives at the grave of Imam Hussain ﷺ, Allah will speak to him confidentially and say, "O My servant! Ask me for anything and I will grant it. Call me, for I will answer you. Desire anything and I will fulfil it and ask Me for any of your needs so that I may grant it." Imam Sadiq ﷺ added, "It is on the Almighty Allah to recompense him for that which he has spent."[96]

3. Imam Sadiq ﷺ is reported to have said:

'Allah has some angels who are appointed at the grave of Imam Hussain ﷺ. When a person decides to perform the Ziyarat of Imam Hussain ﷺ, Allah gives his sins to these angels. With the first step that he takes, the angels will erase his sins and with any additional steps, they will multiply his good deeds until he

---

[95] Kamil Al-Ziyarat, p.252-253
[96] ibid, p.253

becomes eligible for Paradise. Then they will surround him and sanctify him. They will call out to the angels of the heavens, "Sanctify the visitor of the beloved of the beloved of Allah." When the visitor performs the ghusl, Mohammad will call out to him: "Guests of Allah! Glad tiding to you, for you will join me in Paradise." Then Amirul Momineen ؑ will call out, "I guarantee the fulfilment of your requests and to keep afflictions away from you in this life and hereafter." Then the Holy Prophet (saws) will join them and stay to their right and left until they return to their kin.[97]

4. Imam Sadiq ؑ:

'The Almighty Allah records a thousand good deeds and erases a thousand sins for every step taken by one who performs the Ziyarat of Imam Hussain ؑ on foot. He will also increase their status a thousand times for every step. Then Imam said: When you arrive at Euphrates, perform ghusl, carry your shoes and walk barefoot like a humble servant. Once you arrive at the door of the holy shrine, recite Takbeer[98] four times. Then walk a little and repeat this four more times. Then come near his head, stand there and repeat it four more times. Pray near his grave and ask Allah, the Exalted for your needs.'[99]

5. Imam Sadiq ؑ:

'O Ali! Perform the Ziyarat of Imam Hussain ؑ and don't omit it." Ali asked, "What is the reward for one who goes to his Ziyarat?" Imam ؑ replied: Allah will record a good deed and erase a sin for every step taken by one who performs the Ziyarat of Imam Hussain ؑ on foot. He will also add a rank to his rank. When he arrives at the grave, Allah will appoint two angels on him who will only write the good he speaks and not write anything else that he might say or do. When he leaves, they will bid farewell to him and say: "O friend of Allah! You are forgiven. You are from the party of Allah, party of His Messenger and party of Ahlulbayt ؑ of His Messenger. By Allah, you will never see Hellfire and it will never see or burn you.'[100]

---

[97] ibid, p.255-256
[98] That is to say: Allahu Akbar
[99] Kamil Al-Ziyarat, p. 131
[100] ibid, p.132

6. Imam Sadiq ؏:

'Whomsoever visits Hussain ؏ this way (walking), Allah will grant them, for every step, one hundred thousand rewards, and remove one hundred thousand sins, and raise them one hundred thousand levels, and fulfil for them one hundred thousand wants, the easiest of which is removal from hell. They will be considered like those who attained martyrdom with Hussain ؏, sharing with them their statuses.'[101]

The above narrations are only a few of many that have reached us that categorically establish the merit and extensive reward for those who undertake the visitation of Imam Hussain ؏ by foot. This points to the reward being greater by using the foot, compared to other modes of transport. One may wonder why this is the case, and how it could be explained in light of the Qur'an and the Sunnah.

Why is walking to Karbala better than using other means of transport?

Participating in the visitation of the blessed shrine of the grandson of the Prophet, Imam Hussain ؏ is worthy of much reward. The way this Ziyarah is conducted and approached determines the extent of blessings and reward received by the visitor. Scholars have discussed possible considerations behind why walking to Ziyarah has been favoured so much.

In the Holy Qur'an, Allah ﷻ established the obligation of performing the hajj pilgrimage for believers:

وَأَذِّن فِي النَّاسِ بِالْحَجِّ يَأْتُوكَ رِجَالًا وَعَلَىٰ كُلِّ ضَامِرٍ يَأْتِينَ مِن كُلِّ فَجٍّ عَمِيقٍ

'And proclaim the Hajj to people: they shall come to you on foot and on lean camels coming from distant places.'[102]

Several established scholars, such as Fakhr Al-Din Al-Razi[103], Al-Qurtubi[104], and Ayatollah Nasir Makarim Shirazi[105], believe the reason

---

[101] Misbah Al-Mutahajid, p.717
[102] Holy Qur'an (22:27)
[103] Tafsir Al-Kabir, vol.23, p.28
[104] Tafsir Al-Qurtubi, vol.12, p.38
[105] Al-Amthal, vol.10, p.322

'on foot' is mentioned before 'other transport' is the superiority in terms of reward. Some argue people exert more effort when walking; hence, they have been honoured by Allah ﷻ. This is based on Prophetic traditions that point to superiority of more difficult tasks in comparison with easier ones. Wudhu before prayers in the winter is more difficult than the summer, or fasting in the summer is harder than the winter for example. The more effort a believer places in the deed and the more difficult it is to accomplish it, the greater the blessings from the Almighty ﷻ. The same can be said of the walk to Karbala, since one can utilize modern means of transport easily to get to the city. Yet, the millions who walk for days are demonstrating their unswerving loyalty by going through hardship, which is invariably more difficult than simply using cars, for example.

Allamah Hilli has argued that the attaining of *thawab* for every deed is directly proportional to the degree of hardship. In his book Kashf Al-Murad, he contends that, without the necessary difficulty, the reason for reward diminishes.[106] Therefore, by deduction, the virtue of a deed is higher if it includes difficulty for the doer.

Support of the above concept is presented by Imam Baqir ؑ, when describing the conduct of Prophet Mohammad ﷺ. He says:

'When the Prophet was presented with two options, both resulting in the pleasure of Allah, he chose that which was more difficult.'[107] The same description about Imam Ali ؑ is also given by Imam Sadiq ؑ.[108]

When we place these narrations with the one that establishes the superiority of walking in any act of worship of Allah ﷻ, we understand the emphasis placed by the Ahlulbayt ؑ on the walk during Ziyarah.

Imam Sadiq ؑ, in a *(Sahih)* hadith, has said:

'Allah is not worshipped through a greater or better way than by walking.'[109]

This narration points to the importance of walking to perform the deeds that please Allah ﷻ, such as enjoining good relations, seeking

---

[106] Kashf Al-Murad fe Sharh Tajreed Al-Iqtiqad, p. 436
[107] Al-Kafi, vol.8, p.130
[108] ibid, vol.8, p. 163
[109] Wasa'il Al-Shia, vol.11, p.78

knowledge, and praying in a mosque for example. That is why many scholars have commented on the recommendation of walking to hajj, unless it weakens the person from performing other acts of worship.[110]

A well-known Shia Jurist, whose book is taught across the seminaries, is Sheikh Mohammad Hasan Al-Najafi. He is better known as *'Sahib Al-Jawahir'* (the author of Al-Jawahir). In his monumental book of jurisprudence, he says:

'...walking to hajj in humility and submission...is better than other transportation, as is commonly accepted by our scholars...and a similar thing can be said with regards to walking to holy shrines, especially that of my master Abo Abdillah Al-Hussain, and Allah knows best.'[111]

The practice of the scholars

Despite their many commitments, which includes teaching, authoring, and researching, many scholars have undertaken the journey to Karbala on foot. By doing this, even in old age, they set an example for the rest of the believers to emulate. Some scholars, from past and present, who have undertaken the walk to Karbala include:

- Mirza Hussain Al-Nouri

Documenting his journeys to Karbala on foot, Agha Buzurg Al-Tehrani says:

'During the time of Sheikh Al-Ansari, the walk by foot towards the Master of Martyrs was well established. Afterwards, and due to poverty, less people paid attention to it. When our Sheikh noticed this, he paid attention to this issue and became adherent (to the walk). During the visitation of Eid Al-Adha, he would carry his belongings and walk alongside his companions. In his last year...I was honoured to serve the Sheikh who was walking. After the Ziyarah he also returned to Najaf by foot.'[112]

---

[110] Al-Urwat Al-Wuthqa, Vol.4, p.338
[111] Jawahir Al-Kalam fe Sharh Shara'I Al-Islam, vol.17, p.310
[112] Al-Arbaeen wa falsafat al-mashi ila Al-Imam Hussain, p.82

- Allamah Sheikh Abdul Hussain Al-Amini

Al-Hajj Hussain Al-Shakiri narrates:

'He used to visit the master of the youth of Paradise, the Martyr Imam Hussain ﷺ in Karbala walking. This was to obtain more reward. He was accompanied by the best of his friends from the believers, taking 3 or more days (to get there).'[113]

- Ayatollah Sayid Mar'ashi Najafi

One of his students says:

'He told me one day that when he was in Najaf, he was honoured to visit Imam Hussain ﷺ by foot 25 times. He used to undertake this Ziyarah with a group of ten other students, who loved each other for the sake of Allah. They include: Sayid Al-Hakim, Sayid Shahroudi, Sayid Al-Khoei...He (Ayatollah Mar'ashi) said: 'We all became Marajie...and the work during the walk was divided amongst us. Myself and another used to bring water in every place we stopped, whatever it took to do so. Another would prepare food, whilst some prepare tea...Sayid Shahroudi used to say: 'I must instil happiness in your hearts during the journey and make it easier for you.'[114]

- Ayatollah Sayid Abdul A'la Al-Sabzawari

In his biography, one finds:

'At the age of 23, Sayid Sabzawari left walking from Najaf to the sacred land of Karbala to perform Ziyarah of his grandfather the Master of Martyrs.'[115]

- Ayatollah Sayid Mohammad Baqir Al-Sadr

Despite not being able to participate (due to the difficult political situation), Ayatollah Sadr was an ardent supporter of the walk to

---

[113] ibid, p.82
[114] Al-Arbaeen wa falsafat al-mashi ila Al-Imam Hussain, p.83
[115] ibid

Karbala. He offered money to be spent for the visitors of Imam Hussain ﷺ. He wished to join them, and some of his students, like Ayatollah Mahmood Al-Hashemi participated in the walk under the encouragement of Ayatollah Sadr.[116]

- Ayatollah Sayid Mohammad Saeed Al-Hakim

In the last few years, the contemporary marajie have participated in several Arbaeen walks alongside the visitors of Imam Hussain. This was reported by media and his own office.

Similarly, several prominent jurists from Najaf have been seen participating in the walk of Arbaeen. Amongst them is my teacher, Ayatollah Sheikh Mohammad Al-Sanad amongst others.

---

[116] ibid, p.84

Chapter 7:

The Reward of Walking Barefoot for Ziyarah

Taking off the shoes and walking barefoot is seen by many as a sign of humility and respect. When entering holy places of worship, such as mosques, believers are told to remove their shoes. The Almighty ﷻ commands his Prophet Musa ؑ to remove his shoes upon entering the sacred valley of Tuwa:

إِنِّي أَنَا رَبُّكَ فَاخْلَعْ نَعْلَيْكَ ۖ إِنَّكَ بِالْوَادِ الْمُقَدَّسِ طُوًى

'Indeed I am your Lord! So take off your sandals. You are in the sacred valley of Tuwa.'[117]

Imam Ali ؑ also affirms this when asked why it is best to walk barefoot in some places:

'They (specifically) belong to Allah, therefore I love to be barefoot within them.'[118]

Examples where walking barefoot has been recommended

1. The Hajj pilgrimage

Imam Sadiq ؑ is narrated to have said:

'My father informed me from his father that Hasan ibn Ali ibn Abi Talib ؑ was the most devout of the people at his time. He was the most ascetic with highest status. When he went to hajj, he did so walking, or maybe barefoot...'[119]

---

[117] Holy Qur'an (20:12)
[118] Mustadrak Al-Wasa'il, vol.6, p.136
[119] Amali Al-Saduq, p.244

2. Entering Masjid Al-Haram

Imam Sadiq said:

'Upon entering Masjid Al-Haram, be sure to do so barefoot whilst displaying tranquillity and humility.'[120]

3. Walking for Friday prayers

It is narrated that Imam Ali walked barefoot to perform Friday prayers, holding his sandals in his left hand. He said: *'It's a place that belongs to Allah.'*[121]

4. Eid prayers

It is narrated that Imam Redha walked out to perform Eid prayers whilst barefoot.[122]

5. Participating in funerals

Imam Sadiq narrates:

'When Sa'd ibn Ma'ad passed away, the Prophet commanded that he is washed. Thereafter he followed his funeral without sandals or a cloak.'[123]

Similarly, when Ismail, the son of Imam Sadiq passed away, the Imam participated in his funeral without shoes or a cloak.[124]

6. Visiting the sick

A narration from Imam Ali reports he used to walk barefoot when participating in five things:

---

[120] Al-Kafi, vol. 4, p.401
[121] Da'aim Al-Islam, vol.1, p.182
[122] Al-Kafi, vol.1, p.490
[123] Bihar Al-Anwar, vol.78, p.269
[124] Bihar Al-Anwar, vol.78, p.296

'They are places that belong to Allah, and hence I love to be barefoot. The day of Fitr, Day of Adha, Friday, when visiting the sick and taking part in a funeral.'[125]

The basis for the recommendation to be barefoot in sacred places

The main evidence presented is through the Quranic verse (20:12) (stated earlier).

Scholars have agreed that the mention of the words 'sacred valley' indicates the reason of the command to remove the sandals. Therefore, we can infer that any place or land considered sacred will also be included in this category.

The shrines of the Imams undoubtedly come under the umbrella of sanctified places, in which many narrations have pointed to their sacredness and importance. This includes the blessed shrine of Imam Hussain.

Imam Baqir said:

'Allah, the blessed and exalted, created, blessed and sanctified the land of Karbala twenty-four thousand years before He created the Kaaba. Hence it was blessed and sanctified before the creation of any created being and it will remain this way until Allah raises it to Paradise and appoints it as the best land there. It will be the best abode in Paradise in which Allah will make His friends abide.'[126]

A prophetic narration, found in mainly Sunni sources, points to the great benefit of the feet becoming dusted for the sake of Allah:

'Whosoever's feet are dusted for the sake of Allah, the Almighty will make them prohibited from hellfire.'[127]

The contact of the feet with soil or dust is usually more when the human walks barefoot. If the walking is for the sake of Allah, especially in a sacred land, the body will be protected from the fire of hell.

---

[125] Mustdarak Al-Wasa'il, vol.6, p.136
[126] Kamil Al-Ziyarat, Ch. 88, p.289
[127] Sahih Bukhari, vol.2, p. 9. Sunan Al-Tirmidhi, vol.3, p.93, Musnad Ahmad, vol.3, p.367 and more

In terms of the walk to Imam Hussain ؑ's shrine in Karbala, several traditions encourage the visitors to display humility by walking barefoot[128]. For example:

Imam Sadiq ؑ is narrated to have said:

'*When you want to visit Aba Abdillah ؑ, perform ghusl using the Furat. Thereafter wear clean clothes, and walk barefooted since you are in a sacred land that belongs to Allah and His Messenger...*'[129]

The above emphasis should be taken within the context of not causing excessive harm to one's self.

---

[128] The Islamic teachings instruct females to cover their feet as part of the hijab. This does not mean that they will miss out on the rewards of walking barefoot, since by wearing socks they are demonstrating obedience to Allah's commands. If female visitors wish to walk without shoes, they should ensure that the socks are not revealing or see-through.
[129] Al-Kafi, vol.4, p.576

Chapter 8:

Etiquettes of the Walk

1. Sincerity in intention

From the outset, the visitor should establish the sincere intention of performing the walk for the sake of Allah ﷻ. This is critical for the acceptance of the deed. The visitor can perform the walk on behalf of their families or friends. They can include their names at the beginning of the walk and the reward will be attained by them, as well, Insha'Allah.

2. Maintaining ritual purity

It is highly recommended to undertake such acts of worship whilst in state of ritual *tahara* (purity). Hence, the visitor is encouraged to be in *Wudhu* (ritual ablution) at all times and perform the *ghusl* when necessary. Being conscious of this adds to the spiritual experience of the walk and results in more rewards from the Almighty ﷻ.

3. Wearing clean clothes and maintaining personal hygiene

When people visit honourable or respected individuals, they often seek to present themselves in the best possible manner, ensuring personal cleanliness is observed. In the journey to Aba Abdillah, the *za'ir* is encouraged to remember this, noting the traditions that point to cleanliness being a part of faith.

4. Sadaqa and supplication for protection

Throughout any journey, one may face obstacles or possible dangers that may be harmful. It is recommended to ask Allah ﷻ for protection of one's self and others via honest and sincere dua, coupled with charitable donation for the poor - both before and during the walk.

5. Consideration for others

The number of participants in the annual walk to Karbala has increased annually. This has resulted in more congestion during certain points of the walk, especially amongst those starting the walk from the city of Najaf. The visitor to Imam Hussain ﷺ is encouraged to show respect, love, and consideration towards other *zuwwar*. What needs to be remembered is that some have come from distant cities, such as Basra in the south (approximately 500km away!). Others may be villagers, so may not be accustomed to different forms of interaction. Not only should patience and tolerance be shown, for the sake of Allah and in the name of the Master of Martyrs, but respect shown to these individuals as they are the visitors of Imam ﷺ. They occupy a special position in the eyes of the Ahlulbayt.

Pushing, shoving, engaging in arguments or fights, spreading hatred, disrespecting practices or the *marajie* are among the vices that must be avoided.

Instead, the visitor should be motivated to follow in the footsteps of Imam Hussain ﷺ - demonstrating values of altruism, sacrifice, and service to others.

6. Keeping the environment clean

Due to the serving of food and refreshments, which is continuous throughout the walk to Karbala, the roads should be not filled with waste or leftover food thrown away by the walkers. Instead, we should remove any obstacles and be on the lookout for any dangers that may negatively affect or harm the visitors of Imam Hussain ﷺ.

7. Eating moderately and avoiding waste

Throughout the years that I have been blessed to undertake the walk from Najaf to Karbala, I have witnessed the serving of a wide variety of food and refreshments. This includes sweet dishes and fruits. Whilst we may be tempted to try the delicacies, especially as they also include international variations (not just Iraqi), we should not forget the Quranic instruction to not be wasteful nor eat excessively:

وَكُلُوا وَاشْرَبُوا وَلَا تُسْرِفُوا ۚ إِنَّهُ لَا يُحِبُّ الْمُسْرِفِينَ

'…eat and drink, but do not waste; indeed, He does not like the wasteful.'[130]

إِنَّ الْمُبَذِّرِينَ كَانُوا إِخْوَانَ الشَّيَاطِينِ ۖ وَكَانَ الشَّيْطَانُ لِرَبِّهِ كَفُورًا

'Indeed the wasteful are brothers of Satan, and Satan is ungrateful to his Lord.'[131]

Due to their kindness and great willingness to offer food to the *zuwwar*, some of the *mawkibs* exert friendly pressure on the visitors to have food inside their tents or *hussayniyas*. Whilst it is encouraged to respond to the invitation of believers, we must also remember the negative implications upon the soul of excessive eating and being wasteful. We should also recall the difficulty that the caravan of captives endured throughout their journey from Karbala to Kufa and eventually to Sham. Not only was food and water scarce, but they were constantly ridiculed, abused, and had to witness the heads of the martyrs being carried in front of them.

8. Engaging with other believers

Scholars have recommended that travelling by one's self is makruh, and if possible, we should try to join with others during the journey. However, the choice of companions during the walk should centre on positivity and enhancing the benefits from this wonderful journey. For example, it would be encouraging to discuss aspects from Ashura that would intensify the connection with the Imam ﷺ or how one should deal with modern-day challenges as believers.

9. Displaying appropriate mannerisms

As a visitor to Imam Hussain ﷺ, we should be wary of representing ourselves positively and not engaging in behaviour deemed inappropriate in this journey. Gazing at the opposite gender, laughing

---

[130] Holy Qur'an (7:31)
[131] Holy Qur'an (17:27)

loudly, throwing things at each other, shouting at people, ridiculing others, backbiting or slandering believers for example are traits which must be avoided. It is pertinent to remember that the walk will anger Satan, and he will attempt to distract or tempt people into disobedience - which can sometimes start small. In addition, we should seek to protect property and look out for the environment.

10. Applying etiquette of walking

Narrations from the Ahlulbayt ؑ point to walking in humility, not walking fast, and to walk on the side of the road and not in the middle (so as not to attract attention). This is in line with guidelines from the Holy Qur'an:

وَعِبادُ الرَّحمٰنِ الَّذينَ يَمشونَ عَلَى الأَرضِ هَونًا وَإِذا خاطَبَهُمُ الجاهِلونَ قالوا سَلامًا

'The servants of the All-beneficent are those who walk humbly on the earth, and when the ignorant address them, say, 'Peace!''[132]

وَلا تُصَعِّر خَدَّكَ لِلنّاسِ وَلا تَمشِ فِي الأَرضِ مَرَحًا ۖ إِنَّ اللَّهَ لا يُحِبُّ كُلَّ مُختالٍ فَخورٍ

'Do not turn your cheek disdainfully from the people, and do not walk exultantly on the earth. Indeed, Allah does not like any swaggering braggart.'[133]

The Islamic dress code of hijab should be fully observed by the sisters, taking care not to be complacent in this issue. Brothers and sisters should also remember the importance of maintaining social hijab, whereby unnecessary interaction such as laughter should be avoided between *non-mahrems*.[134]

11. Continuous *dhikr* and reflection

The believers will invariably spend at least 8 hours a day walking while taking rests in between. The walk should be utilised for the remembrance of Allah ﷻ, *tasbeeh*, recitation of *salawat*, and reflection.

---

[132] Holy Qur'an (25:63)
[133] Holy Qur'an (31:18)
[134] The non-mahrems are those that according to Sharia Law are not related to each other in a manner which would otherwise allow the female not to observe the hijab from them.

Introspection is crucial, and the time should be spent dedicated to asking hard-hitting questions of ourselves, such as what have I done so far? Where am I heading? Am I ready for the afterlife? How do I improve my situation? How can I get closer to Allah? Such questions, coupled with dhikr, enrich the experience of the spiritual walk. It is also important not to be constantly distracted by the surroundings, and instead meditate silently whilst walking - contemplating the struggles which are a necessary part of life but harbouring a positive mind-set and deliberating practical ways to serve the religion of Islam as desired by the Almighty.

12. *Istighfar* and seeking repentance

When Hur ibn Yazid Al-Riyahi asked Imam Hussain ؑ whether God will forgive him, the response from the Imam was optimistic and full of hope. This serves as an inspiration not to give up in life and not to think (wrongly) that, despite what we may have done, it's too late for repentance. The path to Hussain ؑ is the path to Allah ﷻ, and consequently, genuine and sincere repentance will be accepted by the Almighty, coupled with the determination of the servants not to fall into the transgressions, once again. The lips of the *za'ir* should continuously utter '*Astaghfirulla wa atub ileyhe*[135]', whilst recalling our sins, shedding tears, admitting our shortcomings, and believing the Generous and Merciful Lord will undoubtedly encompass us in His limitless mercy.

13. The displaying of sorrow and grief

Imagine that during the walk, you see the caravan of the Ahlulbayt ؑ taken as captives right beside you. The feeling of pain and sadness will surely overwhelm your emotions, as you see the daughters of the Prophet beaten and dragged across the desert. Recalling the tragedy of Karbala evokes powerful emotions and the shedding of tears has the potential to bring about a tremendous transformation in our lives. This is because tears can bring about softening of the heart. That is why numerous narrations point to the many rewards of those who shed their tears in memory of Ashura, following the life of Prophet Mohammad ﷺ, who cried for Imam Hussain ؑ.

---

[135] Meaning 'I seek God's forgiveness and return in penitence to Him.'

Ahmad ibn Hanbal, the establisher of the Hanbalite Sunni school narrates that Imam Hussain ؏ said:

'Whomsoever eyes cries a drop of tears on us or sheds a single drop of tears on us, Allah will reward him with paradise.'[136]

14. Maintaining prayers

During the Day of Ashura, Imam Hussain ؏ established the Salah, despite the arrows fired at him and his companions from many directions. Throughout the walk, not only should the visitor perform the Salah at the recommended time, and join congregational prayers, but should pledge to prioritise and safeguard their prayers throughout their lives. The walk should ignite the determination not to take prayers lightly and to focus on establishing it whilst seeking an attentive heart.

We should not be distracted by the need to get to a place or position and subsequently delay our prayers. Instead, the moment the *adhan* is recited, the recommended walk should stop for performing the obligatory prayer - our primary obligation and focus should always be the Almighty ﷻ.

15. Prayers and connection with Imam Mehdi (atf)

Whilst walking to the sacred land of Karbala, the visitor is encouraged to pledge their allegiance to the awaited saviour, Imam Mehdi ؏. The living Imam supplicates for the *zuwwar* of his grandfather and seeks forgiveness of Allah ﷻ for them. It is also possible that he joins the *zuwwar* in the mourning rituals and walks towards the city of martyrs. Given the importance of this, it is prudent upon us to remember the Imam, as far as supplicating for his protection and reappearance and performing righteous deeds on his behalf. Supplications, such as *Dua Nudba*, should be recited and pondered over- in particular the following words:

'Is there any way to meet you, O son of Ahmad (the Prophet)?
Will our day be promised to catch your day and we will thus achieve our hope?

---

[136] Fadhail Al-Sahaba, vol. 2, p. 675

When will we be able to join your refreshing springs and we will then be satiated?
When will we quench our thirst from your fresh water, because thirst has been too long?
When will we accompany you in coming and going so that our eyes will be delighted?
When will you see us and we see you spreading the pennon of victory?'[137]

16. Participation in majalis and mourning rituals

The *majalis* of Imam Hussain are a wonderful and regular feature throughout the walk, including the sessions of *ma'tam* (self-beating). No encouragement is usually needed to urge the visitor to partake in these *majalis* as many are themselves yearning to learn and participate in commemoration of the tragedy. Despite the language barrier (although English majalis are organized by the bigger groups and some mawkibs), attendance brings reward and shedding tears demonstrates loyalty.

It is also possible to seek clarification and get answers for questions from the countless stalls throughout the walk looked after by scholars from the seminaries of Najaf and Karbala. Taking shifts, many sit for hours throughout weeks to answer the jurisprudential and theological questions of the visitors.

17. Serving the visitors of Imam

One of the main talking points for those who have undertaken the walk to Karbala are the extensive facilities designed to serve the visitor of Imam Hussain. This is coupled with the spirit of giving by many, especially those in charge of *mawkibs* and *hussayniyas*, ensuring the needs of the visitors are met.

It would be worthwhile (and spiritually rewarding) for the visitor to volunteer at some of these *mawkibs*, seeking to place happiness in the hearts of the lovers of Hussain, but above all, to establish this service for the sake of Allah. Whether its preparing or serving food, providing blankets or mattresses, or offering medical service, the opportunities to attain reward from Allah are many.

---

[137] Mafatihul Jinan, p.342

In recent years, the followers of the Imam from Western countries have established a few *mawkibs*. The opportunity to establish a mawkib is available for those seeking it.

18. Donations and helping the less fortunate

The mind-set of the visitor of Imam Hussain ﷺ should be such that any chance of making an impact upon themselves and others should be capitalised. There are *mawkibs* on the way to Karbala of prominent organisations that look after orphans and the displaced. The opportunity is presented to sponsor orphans or to donate for their housing or education. This form of charity transforms the physical walk into a practical tool for positive contribution to society. Donations and sponsorship of orphans can be done in the name of the children of Imam Hussain ﷺ, such as the 3-year-old Ruqqayah, who endured the torment of Yazid's men throughout the weeks of their journey and was eventually martyred in Damascus.

It is also recommended to donate towards the *mawkibs*, who spend thousands of dollars annually providing food and necessities. I have spoken to a few leading figures in these *mawkibs*, and they have expressed how the costs of maintenance places pressure on themselves and families. Determined to continue, some have resorted to loans or using their savings.

19. Making a pledge to make a change in life

Throughout our lives, the Almighty ﷻ presents us with various stations in which the opportunity for self-development is enhanced. This includes the pilgrimage of Hajj and the Month of Ramadhan. Similarly, the walk of Arbaeen is a glorious occasion to self-reflect and begin a new chapter in our lives. Whether it's the conduct of obligatory deeds, committing sin, or the way in which we interact in society with others, the days of Arbaeen should not end without a commitment or pledge to instigate constructive change within ourselves.

20. Establishing the commitment to be ambassadors of the walk

Many people across the world have most likely not come across the Arbaeen walk and know little about this beautiful demonstration of love and loyalty. It then becomes the responsibility of those who have been granted permission by the Almighty to undertake the journey to become ambassadors worldwide, speaking to Muslims and non-Muslims alike about its appeal and inviting them to participate. It is also crucial to utilise social media, websites, apps, and other means to advance the image of the walk and provide information to the masses. Similarly, people may have misconceptions or have been misinformed about the event. Having experienced it, the visitor is encouraged to inspire family, friends, and others to partake in this journey, dispelling any fears of security or other matters.

Chapter 9:

Useful Tips for the Walk from Najaf to Karbala

The following has been compiled from years of undertaking the walk from Najaf to Karbala. It is not comprehensive but useful as a guideline of the important things to consider.

1. The distance between Najaf and Karbala is approximately 80 Kilometres. The road is marked by numbered poles, from 1 to 1452. The distance between each pole is 50 metres. Covering 20 poles would mean 1 kilometre has been walked. Most people attempt to cover the walk in three days, although some may take longer, since they desire to walk slower or serve at *mawkibs*.

2. People usually start the walk after Fajr prayers, taking regular breaks on the way for food, refreshment, and sleep. Many often settle at a *mawkib* or *hussayniyas* by 7 or 8pm, seeking a place to rest and sleep. Walking at night is also possible and perhaps recommended during the hotter summer months to avoid the excessive daytime heat.

3. Take regular breaks and drink plenty of water to keep hydrated. Avoid over-consumption of food.

4. Before the walk, practice using eastern restrooms as much as possible, since although western style bathrooms are available in some *mawkibs*, they may not be easily found.

5. Pack your essential medicines with you (sufficient for 3 days), with phone chargers and any other essentials. Try to travel light, since food and refreshments will be widely available throughout the walk. Carrying a light back-pack will make the walk easier

and less strenuous. Too often, some pilgrims pack too much and face difficulty carrying their belongings.

6. If not travelling with a group, attempt to secure a place to sleep by 7pm. Many become filled around that time and delay may cause difficulty in finding or being allocated a comfortable location.

7. In terms of footwear, make sure you have 'broken in' to your shoes, selecting comfortable and durable ones. Do not try new shoes at the beginning of the walk.

8. Keep creams such as Vaseline, moisturisers and anti-histamine with you due to the possibility of skin irritation or blisters.

9. Carry an identity card, passport, or group badge and keep it visible. This is important for emergencies. Similarly, ensure you have the details of your accommodation in Karbala with you throughout the walk.

10. It is useful to download the Qur'an, dua, majalis, *ma'tam,* or *marthiya* into your mobile phone or audio player to listen to throughout the walk.

11. It is recommended to take cash with you to donate to the *mawkibs* or charitable organisations throughout the walk.

12. Do not worry about completing the walk or having the physical stamina to do so. If you feel you are not able to keep walking, there are buses that take the *zuwwar* straight to Karbala (usually some traffic is encountered).

13. If you have difficulty sleeping in a large hall due to noise etc., carry earplugs and eye shades to facilitate better sleep and more energy the next day.

14. Avoid drinking water from the plastic cups that many people drink from. Instead, either use the packaged small water

container or water bottles. You may need to keep some with you to be hydrated as there are not many available.

15. Tea is served in many places throughout the walk. Try to drink it using disposable cups, rather than the small glass cups often used. Be aware that Iraqis enjoy very sweetened tea, so don't hesitate to ask for the sugar to be reduced(!).

16. Pick up any litter or obstacles you find on the way that may hurt the *zuwwar* or impede their journey.

17. Consider buying fruit boxes on the way (they are sold by vendors) and distributing it as *sabeel* (donation) for the *zuwwar*. These are often popular and result in *thawab* (reward).

18. Mobile phone reception and internet is usually very limited throughout the walk. This is because of the pressure on the networks owing to the sheer volume of people. You can usually get service before *Fajr* or late at night.

19. Although it is recommended to walk the entire distance, one can participate by walking part of the journey (if unable to walk the whole journey) and attain reward Insha'Allah. The area of *Khan Al-Nus* is approximately halfway through, and it's where some begin the walk.

20. At night and whilst asleep, keep your cell phones hidden and not left to charge at an electrical socket.

21. Check the temperature of the area between Najaf and Karbala a day before and decide on clothing accordingly.

22. Take a small notebook to record any experiences, sights, or stories you come across throughout the walk. You can also do this on your phone.

23. Keep the etiquette of walking in mind (see chapter 8) and ask Allah ﷻ not to make this the last time you undertake this journey.

24. When you see images of scholars or the martyrs, try to recite surah Fateha for their souls and don't forget their families in dua.

Chapter 10:

Recommendations for the Arbaeen Walk

The multi-million people Arbaeen walk has perhaps surprised several people worldwide. The sheer volume of people, both within Iraq and coming from outside the country, increases annually. Despite the growth of this act of worship of Allah ﷻ and the protection of the *zuwwar* by the Almighty, there will invariably be challenges and areas to improve going forward. This will ensure the walk to Karbala is strengthened continuously within the objectives set out by the Master of Martyrs, Imam Hussain ؏. Below are a few suggestions for officials, *mawkib* volunteers, and the visitors to remember and perhaps discuss further.

1. **Maintaining the spirit of Ashura**

Imam Hussain ؏ famously said:

'And surely the aim of my stand is not inspired by vain exultation and it is also not for the quest of kingdom, neither it is to cause dissension and corruption nor it is to wrong anybody unjustly. The purpose of my stand is the reformation of my grandfather's nation. I intend to enjoin goodness and forbid evil. I want to emulate my grandfather, the Holy Prophet ﷺ and my father Ali bin Abu Talib ؏. Whosoever accepts me by accepting the truth, then Allah is higher than the truth. And whosoever rejects me then I will bear patiently until Allah judges between me and them and He is the best Judge.'[138]

With this in mind, everyone involved in any capacity during the Arbaeen walk should seek to implement these golden words into their lives. Specifically, the visitors should be encouraged, through posters, pamphlets, majalis, and other means, the need to seek positive reform of themselves and the community continuously. This should be in line with

---

[138] Maqtal Al-Muqarram, p.108

the teachings of the Qur'an and the Ahlulbayt - as presented by our ulema.

Positive change, at individual, family, and society levels, should be inculcated throughout, and the visitor should be a better individual after the Ziyarah compared to when they set out. The expectation should be that the journey will not be a mere physical movement, but a spiritual path of self-purification and change towards Allah ﷻ.

Practical ways this can be done, for example, is for *mawkib* owners to facilitate prayer reminders and congregational *salah* at *adhan* times. Whilst exerting the special effort to serve food and refreshments to the *zuwwar*, there also needs to be determination to spiritually charge them and get them closer to their faith. This needs time, investment, and training in advance.

2. The PR of Arbaeen

One notable challenge witnessed across the past several years is the lack of worldwide publicity of the millions who walk to Karbala every year. Despite the coverage by predominantly Shia channels and internet sites, much of the world seems unaware of the millions who face possible terrorism to walk for tens of kilometres. People can be forgiven for forgetting that the millions walk in a country which has faced very difficult challenges as far as terrorism is concerned. From the rise of Al-Qaeda to the destruction caused by Daesh (ISIS), the incredible story of Arbaeen in Iraq is unique. Even without the constant threat of suicide bombs or rockets landing anywhere, the march of so many people towards one direction would appeal to people globally.

Yet, despite the spectacular nature of the Arbaeen walk, not enough work has been put in to enhance the publicity to the world and introduce it to non-Muslims. Major TV networks, such as CNN or the BBC, rarely cover the Arbaeen walk or send reporters. The same can be said about well-known newspapers, such as Washington Post or The Times. To date, we have seen no major news corporation produce a documentary or satisfactory report about the millions walking to Karbala. This is despite the fact that this event has now happened annually for over ten years.

A programme of publicity should be designed, funded, and supported by directors and officials of the blessed shrines in Iraq to broaden coverage of the Arbaeen walk. The correct communication and contact should be established with the media, providing the security and other arrangements to cover the Arbaeen walk comprehensively. This includes facilitating security, accommodation, interviews, logistical arrangements and anything else necessary to encourage media participation and coverage.

Chapter 11:

Personal Experiences of the Walk to Karbala

The following are some stories of personal experiences by some who were privileged to undertake the walk to Karbala across the last few years. Some of the names were withheld due according to individual requests.

The Journey to Paradise

A journey of lovers. The longest dining table in the world. An all-inclusive resort in the midst of the arid, scorching Iraqi desert. These are just some descriptions attributed to the mesmerising walk from the cities of Najaf to Karbala to mark the occasion of Arbaeen (the fortieth).

For Muslims and non-Muslims across the world, Hussain (grandson of Prophet Mohammad and son of Ali and Fatima) serves as a saintly figure, who constantly reminds them to better themselves and try to influence society positively. Millions commemorate the fortieth day after his death anniversary every year by flocking to his shrine in Karbala. This pilgrimage, widely recognised as the single largest annual peaceful gathering in the world, is one where swarms of people walk united to pay allegiance to a man who left an everlasting legacy 1400 years ago – one that would inspire many generations after his death. Children waddle with parents, the elderly venture in wheelchairs – even the disabled hobble along, step-by-step, supported by nothing but crutches and an iron will to voyage to salute Hussain. One aged lady from southern Iraq hopped into a wheel-barrow and called on people to push her along until they got tired. She knew she'd make it to Karbala nine days later to visit Hussain – and she would not have it any other way.

Leaving the holy city of Najaf, where Hussain's father and guide, Ali ibn Abu Talib, is buried, you then begin a three-day journey on foot guaranteed to change your life. At first, particularly as a Westerner, you feel disorientated by the thought of walking for days on end, through a desert in war-torn Iraq, but this feeling of anxiety quickly fades at the sight of the million-strong crowd (if not more) of fellow walkers. 2013 was my first visit to Iraq. For some time, I had vowed the first time I visited Hussain would be after having done this walk. As advised, I packed a small rucksack with a couple of spare clothes, deodorant, some snacks, and thermal wear – I was warned about how cold it could get in the night! Alas, there was no need to pack anything. Along the journey, one finds tents (called *mawkibs*) established by the locals to serve the visitors of Hussain (known as *zuwwar*) with an abundance of facilities and amenities.

The menu typically includes soup, falafel (served best with a tangy orange sauce), rice dishes, and plenty of fruit. Water is in endless supply, and every minute you will find a stand serving the renowned "chai abu Ali" – fresh, sweet, hot tea to keep energy levels high (it's a case of how much tea you want to take with your sugar, rather than the other way around!). There are people on hand to massage your feet and legs, buildings where you can rest and charge your phone, people to fix your pram or Zimmer frame, fresh clothes provided if needed, places to shower, and lots of public toilets. Once sunset nears, the 'people-motorway' quietens down, and there are numerous tents to sleep in. At these hostels, you are provided with a mattress, pillow, and very cosy blankets.

So, how much money should you take with you to pay for this wonderful hospitality? None. The currency on this walk is servitude and kind-heartedness. Every volunteer you encounter will be more grateful to the visitor than vice-versa, for it is the biggest honour to aid and attend to the guests that make this journey. Once you realise this, your heart will melt, and you appreciate the Godly values of peace and harmony Hussain's legacy has left.

Everyone who has been on this walk will have a story to tell you, so allow me to share mine. As I got split up from my group and I neared Karbala, admittedly, I was tiring and perhaps, it was showing; a stocky Iraqi man grabbed me from the crowd and sat me on a bench. Speaking in a local dialect, which I couldn't understand, he removed my shoes and socks for me. I was startled. I noticed what looked like a metal trough, in which there was thick, soapy-looking water. The man gently caressed warm water on my feet whilst massaging them, as I sat speechless and embarrassed that an elder would do this for me. As I watched him smile and thanked God for allowing him to wash my feet, I could only well up with tears and kiss his forehead, thanking God for letting me partake in this mesmerising trip.

Only a few kilometres later, I wondered the time and when and where to stop for afternoon prayers. A man was shepherding people into a building for supplication and welcomed me in with a gleaming, warm smile. Greetings of peace, smiles that reached our eyes, and contentment were enough to communicate with the Iranian man I prayed next to. Both of us knew we were only half an hour away from the glorious destination of the shrines of Hussain and his brother Abbas. After praying, I looked to exit from the hall, but was quickly made to sit down again. It was lunchtime. Having eaten a falafel only an hour ago, food was the last thing I wanted. The initial brother who welcomed me in stood near me and urged me to eat. There were five volunteers and about two hundred people, yet his attention was solely on me. Some of the local volunteers looked at me, wondering if I was someone special (with my thick British accent and Nike joggers, I must have looked a fair bit off the beaten track). I insisted I couldn't eat the tray of food given to me and agreed to have the orange and water. Not feeling content that he'd served me enough, the man offered me accommodation in Karbala. After I politely declined, he offered me financial help – which again, I respectfully declined. Finally, he gestured to get me a fresh T-shirt – he felt honour-bound to fulfil some act of compassion or service so his role as a host would be fulfilled.

Now, I don't know what the word for this behaviour is – but generosity doesn't seem to cut it. Where else on the planet does one find such selflessness (and to a stranger no less)? What I know is that the three-day journey is filled with moments like this, whereby there is absolutely no doubt that Hussain warms every heart and inspires people to new heights of compassion.

Approximately 80km, three days, and hundreds of cups of tea later, with tired legs, and a heart bursting with emotion, my eyes fell on the illustrious, golden dome of Hussain's shrine. Joy, sadness, humility, and honour all amalgamate into a stream of tears, for paradise on earth had been reached.

Anonymous

The Addictive Walk

When I started the walk 5 years ago, I got addicted, and since then, I do not miss the walk. It's addictive because of hospitality of Iraqis and the Spiritual enhancement.

Mohammad Ladak (Moshi, Tanzania)

The Decisive Moment

I was given the opportunity to go for Ziyarat to Karbala in December 2014 with my family. My family was going for the walk from Najaf to Karbala, but I had decided not to join them for the walk due to my knee pain.

On the day of the departure, when everyone had gathered in the hotel of the lobby- the atmosphere was electric. The lobby was crowded with the walkers and the relatives who had gathered to see them off. The flag bearer was ready, and the instructions were given out.

Some well-wishers, who were non-walkers, had gathered to see their relatives off, hugging each other and bidding farewell until they all met up in Karbala. Some of the non-walkers were feeling sorry for themselves, as they couldn't join their relatives on the walk due to their own personal issues.

I was one of them! I met a lady in remission from cancer, and she told me she was doing the walk but for only one day. By that time- the group had already stepped out of the hotel door.

I started thinking fast, saying that if she can do it, why can't I? Also, if I don't do the one day walk, I might regret it for the rest of my life. Who knew if I would get such an opportunity again? I told my friends "I must do it." They agreed and motivated me to go and said not to give it a second thought. So I rushed out of the door with not even a bag or any warm clothes. Someone from the crowd lent me a jacket (it was cold), and someone else lent me her warm scarf on my way out. All the time, I was wondering what I would do if I couldn't find my group, as it was a good 7 minutes since they had left.

Luckily, I saw them nearby and joined them, and my relatives couldn't believe their eyes when they saw me! That was the best decision of my life ever! I am so glad I went. It is an unforgettable experience that must be done to believe it! Believe me- my knee issue disappeared magically. I experienced no knee pain. Things just fell into place automatically- the walk, the food, the sleep, the zawars, even if it was for one day only.

I have not had the opportunity to go for the walk again, and I am so thankful to the inspiration from Allah and the Imams; otherwise, I would have regretted it for my whole life if I hadn't gone.

Saira Walji

The Real Experience of a lifetime

You must have heard 'it's an experience of a lifetime' and it is! You must have also heard 'everyone should make this journey at least once in their life to experience it' and you must! You can hear about it from everyone around you, and you can see pictures and videos, but you can only experience it when 'you' undertake this journey. It will not be the same for everyone, and you may not feel the same feelings as everyone else, and that is perfectly okay.

It is a journey of self-reflection. There are some who know clearly why they were invited by the Imam to undertake this journey, whilst others, like me, have pondered the reason to be invited, throughout the trip. Some may find their answers there, whilst others will still dwell on this question long after they come back.

You must do the walk. If you can't do the full walk, you must do a one day walk, at least. It may not be the same as the full walk, but you should experience the outpour of love in the name of Imam Hussain ؏ in many forms.

For the Walk:

It is mind over body. Often (especially for first timers), your body will tell you "this is it. I can't go any further", and if you look for signs, there will be lots around you that will boost your energy every time you feel like giving up. You will see old people on walking sticks, people on crutches (some have lost their legs), people on their arms and knees, young children, males, females. The walk is for everyone, regardless of age, race, ethnicity, gender, healthy or not, wealthy or not. There is no division. You must have a strong mind to help you keep going. Besides that, an encouraging partner is a bonus, but don't despair if you're going by yourself. You will be blessed with great company, or you may find solace in being alone. The journey is miraculous! Sometimes, you will witness it whilst being part of it, and other times, you will realize it in hindsight.

Request:

Please do not litter! Regardless of how the city and country is set up, i.e., the locals and everyone else around you will litter left, right, and centre. I request you to not forget your duties as a Muslim. There are trash cans everywhere. Find one to throw your trash in. Hold it for a few minutes until you find one, but for Imam Hussain (as)'s sake, please do not litter. That is one thing that broke my heart every time. I would cringe every time I'd see someone littering. It is one thing when they litter. They will have to clean it up, but you, as a Muslim, should not feel you must add to the trash. Do not forget your values just because you are not at home and will not be cleaning up. This IS Home. Home is where the heart lives, and if your heart lives in Karbala, it is home. You may not be cleaning up, but imagine if it's the Imam cleaning up after you! Who knows?

Please do clean up after yourself - be it after eating, using the bathroom, or any space you occupy. Whether you are sharing with others or not, I cannot stress this enough for the *zuwwar* of Imam Hussain (as).

Anonymous, Florida, US

The awe-inspiring service

I was walking along the road when I came across a group of young people sitting near the curb. I could see they were working hard, covered in dust, and rapidly cleaning and polishing the shoes of the *zuwwar* of Imam Hussain ﷺ. As I passed by them, one of the young boys of the group stood up and grabbed my hand. He motioned towards my feet and said something in Arabic, which I presume was a request to polish my shoes. I refused and thanked him for his kindness, but he would not take no for an answer. He did not let go of my hand and guided me to where his friends were sitting and took my shoes off, despite my repeated refusals. They had my shoes cleaned and polished in less than a minute, and while they were cleaning, they were reciting *latmiyyas* and *zikr* of Aba Abdillah ﷺ. I was absolutely awe-struck at how sincere and loving these people were. They could have been doing so many other things, but they all decided to be at this spot during the walk of Arbaeen, cleaning the shoes of complete strangers! May Allah bless the people of Iraq.

Khuddam e Abbas

The Sweet Pain

Alhamdulillah, I have been blessed to go to Karbala for the past 7 years for Arbaeen, and I pray to Allah to give me the chance to go there every year to perform my Ziyarat e Arbaeen. Last year, I walked from Najaf to Karbala with my mum. My mother had severe pain in her left hand, but we still walked and left all our pain aside as our pain is nothing compared to the pain of Aba Abdillah.
We started our walk on the 15th November 2016 at 1pm after Zohrain Salah, and by 6pm, we reached pole 300 and slept there for 6 hours. My mum's hand pain increased, and she could barely sleep. So, we started our walk midnight 1am. We walked for Imam Hussain only. It felt like the land was folding at one time; we saw we were at pole 600, and we walked, and other time, we saw we were already at pole 800. It was nothing but pure miracle. Imam Hussain helped us. We reached in our hotel at 11pm, shocked, wondering how on earth this could have happened? Seeing the dome of Abulfazl made me realise that, yes, it's him who was with us and helping us.
Once in your lifetime visit Karbala, walk only for Imam Hussain. Imagine his pain, imagine Imam Zainul Abideen's pain when your

shoulder hurts carrying the heavy bag. He carried chains and walked miles with the pain. Why can't we bear that pain for just 3 days!

Ya Allah grant us Ziyarat of Imam Hussain every year!!!

Zuwwar Hussain

Remembering the Thirst

Everyone comes back from visiting Aba Abdillah, sharing with me their special moments of depth and clarity that only the heart and soul can truly comprehend.

Here is my story: On the third and final day of our walk from Najaf to Karbala, the sunrise felt special. Today was the day we arrive in Karbala, the moment we were all waiting for. The first time, I got to visit these golden domes. Thinking of the last 2 days and 20 hours of walking, I was in awe I had made it this far. The generosity of the Iraqis and volunteers serving us every step of the way was heart-warming. Every so often, there would be people passing out plastic sealed cups of water. The first few times I waited for everyone to have water before I went up to the box, because it made me happy to see their smiles after sipping the cold water. The water always gone, so I tried waiting until I needed the water to drink it. The next person serving water came up, and I thought, okay, I will take water this time. I went, many hands reaching in, and there was a few left, but when I reached to grab a cup, they were gone. Beside me, there were 2 little boys, 4 and 7 years of age, who also reached into the container for water. As I continued walking, about 6 steps later, I felt a tug at my abaya. I turned around to see the two little boys who handed me their water, smiling with arms stretched out to me, obliging me to take it. I smiled, and my heart sank as I shook my head to say "it's okay", but they continued to insist and smile, saying "lotfam, lotfam ya zuwwar Hussain", or 'please, please dear visitor of Hussain'. I couldn't hold back my tears. Sobbing, I took the water and thanked the two children. That moment of clarity. The spark inside of my heart. I was thinking, these small children, who barely even have sandals on their feet, probably need the water more than me. But they give it away so freely; what generous hearts these are! What young beautiful souls with such character, so content with nothing and pleased with everything! I want to live life this way. What am I living for? Where am I going? I'm going to Hussain, the man who died thirsty while he fed even his enemies and their horses water before they trampled on his body...

Fatima Sohawon

The Journey of Life

We started our spiritual walk on Thursday at around 4am to Karbala. We began with 18 people and ended up in a group of 4. People I have never met before. But we stayed together for 3 full days until we reached our destination in Karbala.

We continued our walk until pole 530, where we came across this beautiful bungalow and we rested for the night. My legs were hurting a lot, but thank God, no blisters. We prayed Maghreb jamaat Salah, asked for permission to sleep indoors, and I crashed for the night. I felt a fever coming.

I woke up at around 12 midnight to a dark room with people all around me. The night was chilly outside, and I noticed people sleeping in blankets outside in the freezing cold. God bless them. I went back in after using the toilet and slept until Fajr time. We all woke up, prayed Salah, and continued with our walk Friday early morning.

My right ankle got stiff, and eventually, I used a stick (which was generously donated by a soldier) to help me walk. The walk was beautiful with so many friendly people without an ounce of pride. Everyone shared the same feelings and goal. They all had the love of Hussain in their hearts. The locals were very giving and fed you continuously during your walk. It didn't matter where you came from.

We stopped to pray jamaat Dhuhr Salah on the side of the road with hundreds of people. It was a great feeling to be amongst people of your own true faith. This represented my congregational prayers for the day. I noticed that, everywhere we stopped, the jamaat Salah was always Qasr. People were all in transit, just like we are in this world.

We continued to pole 1086 (WF Mawkib) and rested for the night there. We got four spaces, even though it was crowded.

We had a wholesome breakfast on Saturday morning with halwa puri, paratha, tomato omelette, bateta curry, chole, and chai. I took a patch of salon pas and applied it on my ankle (which became immobile overnight). I was ready to walk on my knees if I had to. Alhamdulillah, all the brothers, assisted in carrying my backpack and gave me a helping hand. God bless them all. We reached our hotel safely on Saturday at around 3pm. Alhamdulillah, what a blessed journey.

It's amazing the vibe and energy during the walk, the people you meet that you may never meet again. The gifts they leave you, one only wonders who sent them to you.

This was a journey of life. You come across all kinds of people originating from across the world headed towards the same destination. On that road, you will give help; you will get help. You will bond with some and continue your journey with them. You will remember all that you have done through your life and ask for forgiveness for all your sins, hoping you will be forgiven. You get pain but try to bear it for the fruits that lie ahead. One also wonders how all the people serving the zuwwar are sustaining their expenses, as it would cost millions of dollars to feed the millions of people walking daily. An invisible hand for sure... and angels.

Nothing can ever prepare you for this walk, no matter what precautions you take beforehand. But with the love and the will to meet our beloved Imam, you will get the help and strength to finish it. You can never get lost in this journey, since the road and destination are the same. Leave all your worries to Allah, and you will be guided.

The journey took us exactly 3 days, starting on day 1 before Fajr and ending on day 3 at Asr time. Imam Hussain (as) was without water and endured a battle for those same 3 days, yet we complain about pain? Ours is absolutely nothing in contrast. I thank Allah for the opportunity granted to do this blessed walk. I don't know when I will have the chance to do it again.

Arif Jacksi

The Humble Walk

The world's largest annual public gathering. The journey of the lovers. The walk of the free. The longest dining table/path on earth. A life changing experience. These are just a few descriptions attributed to the fascinating walk taking place in the war-torn Iraq, from the city of Najaf to Karbala on the occasion of Arbaeen. Hussain, the man who inspires humanity 1400 years later, the man that enables humanity to better themselves through his practices and examples, the man that fought for justice, right and freedom against 10,000 with a group of 70 only, this man left a legacy centuries later and is the reason millions flock towards his shrine every year to commemorate the 40th day after his death. The journey involves millions of people from various backgrounds, nationalities, and cultures, each marching towards Aba Abdillah with their own perception, challenges, and most of all, their main purpose for experiencing this all-inclusive resort on the desert of Iraq. Allow me to share my personal experience and thoughts about this very mesmerising journey that I've been on for 3 years now, Alhamdulillah.

As a frequent visitor of Aba Abdillah on various occasions during the year, i.e., Arafat, 15th Shaban, Eid Ghadeer and Laylatul Qadr, the feeling of being on the holy plains during Arbaeen was incomprehensible. When the walk was first introduced and known to me, I made up my mind, right away, from that very year, if I was in Iraq for Arbaeen, I would not reach Aba Abdillah any other way than the walk, and this came without experiencing or even being aware of the process. However, the first year I made it to Iraq for Arbaeen, I made it just in time for the Arbaeen night due to my examinations at University; hence, the walk did not happen. This left me very saddened throughout the trip, and every time I heard someone talk about it or the very moment I stepped foot into the courtyard of Aba Abdillah and Abal Fadhl, a voice in me kept crying and yearning to have been part of the walk. However, I convinced myself and was grateful for even having made it on the holy plains for Arbaeen. After that, every year, as I bend down to tie my shoelaces, I mentally brace myself for a three day walk of the free.

I begin the journey in high spirits as I watch millions from all over the world joining me, as together, we mark the walk as the largest, yet peaceful, gathering in the world. I watch in awe as locals warmly offer us food, massages, and resting places, despite their poverty. I'm overwhelmed as I see young children happily distributing fruits and water, as the elderly serve us tea and a variety of foods. Love and generosity are overflowing amid these people. On my first walk, various thoughts crossed my mind, like how much money will I need, what to pack, what snacks to carry, will it be warm enough sleeping in the mawkibs and so forth. However, as I started the walk with a friend I met in Najaf a few days ago and realised the purpose of the experience, I realised I did not need any of the stuff I was thinking of; this immediately reminded me of why the walk is called 'the walk of the free' by others.

On our third day as we were approaching Karbala, admittedly, we were tired and were looking to stop every few minutes. We then randomly stopped by a *Mawkib* to stretch our feet, and some ladies walked out to welcome us inside their house. Their smiles and their warm gestures of initiating a conversation, even though we were not that great at speaking Arabic, literally took our mind of the thought we were in agony and looking for somewhere to rest. We walked in and tried to speak to the girls and two young ladies that then offered us a leg massage. We were startled for a second, as that is all we were looking for throughout the walk, somewhere to heal our feet. I was left speechless at how the Imam takes care of us during the walk. The nature of the Iraqi people during the walk is truly the only thing that gets you through this mesmerising walk. Words don't do justice to their service, love, care, and beautiful nature with the power to win a million visitors (*zuwwar*). As we were approaching the holy plains of Karbala, various speakers in our group (Spiritual Journeys) mentioned the significance of sighting the dome for the first time, and how Aba Abdillah never turns down the first three wishes at first glance.

As I approached the courtyard of Aba Abdillah, my heart burst with emotions as my eyes fell on the illustrious, golden dome. The words of the speakers were engraved in my mind, and every year from the first year, on completing the walk, my first wish on sighting the dome was for Aba Abdillah to grant me visitation and the ability to be part of the walk every Arbaeen. The fact that I've been part of the walk for three consecutive years is a proof that Aba Abdillah never turns down his *zuwwar*. Many people often ask me what it's like to be in Iraq during Arbaeen; however, words never do justice to the feeling of being in paradise on earth. That is the most perfect way to describe it. I'd urge every lover of Aba Abdillah to make it a point to visit Iraq and be part of the fascinating walk during Arbaeen, for one cannot miss the opportunity of experiencing what heaven on earth is.

Sayyada Hassanali

The Safe Haven

We'd already gone two days without a shower or a meal satisfying our taste buds. We were anxiously looking forward to pole 1086. It was late when we trudged into the *mawkib* (camp), but the kind volunteers hurriedly altered their medical camp room into a sleeping room for the other *zuwwar* (travellers) who were still trickling in. It didn't take us long to knock out for the night, the first full rest we got since leaving home (excitement was abuzz in Dubai and Najaf). We'd woken up bright and early to begin the last day of our walk (and clear out the room, so the medical supplies could be brought back in). A hot breakfast, bandaged blisters, and a few hours later, we were ready to go. God had other plans. One thing after another and our departure was pushed back to after the afternoon prayers.

We sat on the plastic sheet laid out behind the main building, waiting for our group to be ready, using this time to people-watch. Throngs of them walked in through the gates, children, adults, seniors in wheelchairs.

Several sat around us. We watched these kids, the boys anyway, pick up their grandmother's walking sticks, get into position, and pretend to shoot into the sky. My sister and I stared, appalled. They were barely six years old. Why were they showing so much violence? We did some quick math. That's ALL they've ever seen. They'd been born years after their country was torn apart by war and just before more terrorism engulfed their homes. We looked into the sky, where they pointed the walking stick/gun. It was a tan helicopter, a news or security one, likely. From the little Arabic I understood, one boy said to the other in a raspy voice "You cover that side. I'm taking care of them." Protection of their family. At 6. Our eyes glistened and cheeks moistened. Their childhood had been snatched away from them. But this wasn't it.

I turned towards Saamiya, nudging her to look towards my left. A young woman, about my age probably, fixed her scarf in a shard of mirror, perhaps the size of two finger tips. We remembered we had a brand-new mirror recently gifted to us that we'd brought to fix our own scarves during the walk (we found we had zero time for that). We slid it to her. She refused profusely. We insisted. A little negotiation later, she agreed, thanked us with the most genuine smile, and admired the pretty patterns on the cover of the mirror. We'd made some of many friends.

The elder woman, the boys' grandmother, pointed towards me and said I reminded her of her sister, whilst the other women in her group agreed in their hurried, natural dialect. Now, we'd made some friends. We spoke for a few minutes, shared snacks with the kids, and exchanged plans for the rest of the journey. Ours were much more elaborate; luxurious is an understatement on its own.

We checked the time and peeked to the other side to see if our group was ready. Their backpacks were on, and their shoes were tied. We knew our time with this family was up. We wished them farewell and asked to take a picture. The little girl seemed scared to stand in front of the camera, so all of us stood together.

The farewell was a little long... culture is such. And what the grandmother told me next made me grateful my shades were still covering my eyes. I asked her to repeat herself as my Arabic is poor.

A tear trickling down her own cheek, she repeated, "Their father (pointing to the kids) has fled Daesh (ISIS) in hopes to reach England and maybe bring us over. His life was in danger, and they kept knocking at our doors to get him. We hope to join him soon or that he comes back to us. Please pray to God (in the shrines in Karbala) these evil Satans are punished, so we can have peace in our country."

Forever bashful for the complaints I make waiting in the 'citizens'' line of my home countries. Forever praying for this world to be a haven for all; for when we see our world from outer space, there are no borders that separate one 'superior' nation from another.

Sumayya Pirbhai

The Warm Relief

My first Ziyarat to the Ahlulbayt was in Arbaeen. I remember being exhausted by the walk in those cold December nights. I was accompanied by my mother, who walked the first day but couldn't carry on for the rest. She was transported to the hotel. I remember, when I finally got to the precinct of the shrines, I lost our group heading towards Hazrat Abbas's shrine; instead, I got redirected to Imam Hussain. I knew my mother wanted to meet him, but I was too tired, and without the recommended ghusl, I then tried to find the hotel. I was lost. I kept praying Surah Al Qadr until I found someone from our group from their name tag on the back. I proceeded towards the hotel like an injured patient. My health deteriorated, and I was sick the whole night. Even though back at home I had done half marathons, I was ill by the walk. All I could think was of Imam Zayn Al Abideen. The next day was eve of Arbaeen. I could barely leave my hotel room. I felt awful that I couldn't participate. At night, when everyone was gathering to leave to visit the shrine, I wanted to go. My mum advised me not to, but I couldn't let myself not go after all the effort in travel to visit this place at this special day. My mother gave me her big full coat to keep warm. She still wasn't happy in me going. I stepped outside, walked a little, and then the next thing I knew, someone tall with clothes fit for a battle was reaching towards me and hugging me. My instinct told me this was Abu Fadhl Al Abbas ﷺ. It was a warm hug, and I felt my illness had went away. Next thing I knew, I had about 10 people looking at me and someone saying, 'He is waking up.' I realised I hadn't left far from the hotel and had fainted. I realised then that I didn't need to walk and visit the shrine to qualify for an acceptance from the Leader of Martyrs. I reached my hotel room to find my mother also reading Ziyarah Arbaeen (from a distance). As I told her about the incident, she said your Ziyarah is already acknowledged.

Ali Asad Jaffrey

The Special Invitation

I saw a post on Facebook on the importance of going for the walk to Karbala, but due to financial constraints, I posted 'if only money grows on trees.' Amazingly, the next day, I was contacted by a person whom I did not know, who told me he wanted to pay for the tickets for my entire family to go to Iraq! I was amazed, and a few weeks later, I landed in Baghdad airport. Everything was working out, and in the walk, I felt like I was being treated like a King. Imam Hussain ﷺ. took care of everything. When I entered Karbala, I felt the city of tranquillity and peace. The dome was beautiful. The city was full of life and blessings because of Imam Hussain ﷺ. I felt at peace. It was the most beautiful place on earth. I felt like entering Paradise, when I entered the shrine of Imam Hussain ﷺ. It was so overwhelming.

Yassin Rashid

The Powerful City

Karbala is often called 'the land of tears'. Thousands of years ago, tears of grief flowed through the land, but today, Karbala is the land of love. Not the love that one has for family and friends, but the love that one can have only for the Ahlulbayt. During my Ziyarat, I experienced many types of love: loss, sacrifice, peace, and hope.

Often, when we embark on journeys to holy places, we naturally make dua for ourselves and our loved ones. Sometimes, we may forget to mention our Muslim brothers and sisters suffering in our duas. Iraq is a country that has been under oppression and war for decades. Loss of life is not uncommon. While traveling throughout the country, I couldn't help but notice the many banners of Iraqi men, young and old, who became martyrs in the fight against terrorism. Everywhere I went, there were armed men in uniform patrolling the streets and shrines. These were students, doctors, clerics, teachers, ordinary people who left their families to protect the holy sites because of their love for the Ahlulbayt ﷺ. It is the sacrifice of these men, past and present, who make it possible for us to perform Ziyarat safely.

As I walked through each holy mosque paying my respects to our Imams, their families, and companions, I reflected on the peace I felt in these majestic shrines. Embellished ceilings, golden domes, shining chandeliers, floral scents, and intricate silk rugs reflect the aesthetics of heaven. The awe inspiring physical beauty of these sites is to honour them in this world. After leaving the shrine of Imam Hussain ﷺ, I looked around and saw children playing in the mosque courtyards, families sharing meals, and bazaars bustling with shoppers. How could a place of immense tragedy and pain now be a beautiful sanctuary? Did the 72 men who became martyrs and the brave women who lost their dignity on the Day of Ashura even imagine they would be honoured after all these years?

This love is protecting the holy lands of Najaf and Karbala from modern day tyrants and oppressors. Love led Imam Hussain to make the greatest sacrifice to preserve the religion of his grandfather, our beloved

Prophet. After experiencing these different types of love, I left the holy land of Karbala with hope for our ummah and a deeper love for the Ahlulbayt. I asked myself, what will be my sacrifice for humanity?

Parisa Kharazi

Chapter 12:

Etiquettes of Ziyarah

Many acts of worship in Islam are presented with several recommendations to enhance the spiritual experience and gain maximum blessings.

Whilst recognizing the importance of these graves and the significance of Ziyarah, the visitor is encouraged to practice and apply the *Adaab* (*etiquettes*) that will undoubtedly help with the fulfilment of the spiritual and physical benefits of this noble act. These include:

1. Sincerity

The intention should be purely to seek the satisfaction of Allah ﷻ alone. The visitor must be careful not to perform the Ziyarah to show off to others or to boast about this blessing. The purer the intention, the greater the Divine blessings and mercy.

2. Physical purity

The Quranic message is to enter the places of worship both in purity and in good presentation. In the Quranic verse (7:31), Allah ﷻ commands:

...خُذُوا زِينَتَكُم عِندَ كُلِّ مَسجِدٍ...

'*...put on your adornments in every mosque...*'

When approaching the shrines of the Ahlulbayt ﷺ, the visitor should recognise that Allah ﷻ has purified and cleansed them thoroughly; therefore, visiting their site entails a degree of physical purity.

The visitor should remain in Wudu and in a state of purity whilst in these holy places. Performing ghusl (ritual wash) before the visit, especially on the first occasion, has been mentioned in countless narrations. The wearing of clean and pure clothes and putting on perfume is also recommended. However, the latter (perfume) is not recommended when visiting the shrine of Imam Hussain ﷺ.

3. Manner of approaching

The visitor is advised to walk to and inside the shrine with humility and reverence. While remembering the greatness of the individual being visited, the believer is encouraged to enter calmly and with a peaceful heart. Shoes and sandals should be removed, and steps should be shortened. Throughout the journey towards the shrine, and inside, the visitor is encouraged to purify their lips with the remembrance of Allah ﷻ and salutations upon the Holy Prophet and his pure family. Imam Al-Sadiq ﷺ encourages the visitors to observe this etiquette:

'When you are going towards Aba Abdillah, peace be upon him, perform a ghusl in the tributary of [the River] al-Furat, then put on clean clothes and walk barefooted as indeed you are in a sanctuary of the sanctuaries of Allah and of His Messenger, and thus I advise you to continuously magnify Allah (Allahu Akbar) and sanctify Allah (La ilaha illa Allah), the veneration of Allah (Subhan Allah); the praise of Allah (Alhamdulillah); and the ennoblement of Allah (Subhan Allah Al-Atheem) – the Glorious and Majestic, and by sending prayers and salutations upon Mohammad and his family (reciting the Salawat) and continue in this way until you reach the door of the shrine.'[139]

4. Seeking permission to enter

Before entering a holy shrine or cemetery, the visitor is urged to seek permission from Allah ﷻ, His Messenger, the Imam, and the angels. This has been established widely through various supplications and refers to the concept that the Holy Prophet and the Ahlulbayt ﷺ hear the permission and respond, despite us not perceiving it. It affirms the sacredness of the shrine and the idea of it being a place of sanctity and

---

[139] Al-Kafi, vol.4, p.575

guidance. The seeking of permission to enter is a Qur'anic recommendation:

يَا أَيُّهَا الَّذِينَ آمَنُوا لَا تَدْخُلُوا بُيُوتَ النَّبِيِّ إِلَّا أَن يُؤْذَنَ لَكُمْ

'O you who have faith! Do not enter the Prophet's houses unless permission is granted you…'[140]

While verbally asking for permission, it is recommended that the visitor feels a sense of humility in their heart, asking themselves whether they are deserving of permission being granted. Shedding tears and expressing thankfulness for this blessing is also advised.

At the entrance, it is prudent to enter using the right foot, whilst reciting *takbeer* (Allahu Akbar). Taking short steps, whilst humbly lowering the head, is also recommended.

5. Remembrance of Allah

Inside the holy shrine, engaging in worship and remembrance of the Almighty is highly desirable. This can be through *Salah*, Quran recitation, *istighfar* (seeking forgiveness), *tasbeeh* (glorification), or *dua* (supplication).

6. Seeking the blessing of the shrine

The visitor is recommended to display his love towards the holy personality buried in the shrine by kissing the doorway and the mausoleum. It is one way of showing respect to this blessed area. The Holy Quran informs us that objects that come in contact with a holy individual are a source of healing, for example, the shirt of Prophet Yusuf. Many Muslims also kiss the cover of the Holy Qur'an when they come across it or upon reciting it. This is not tantamount to worship of these objects, but a demonstration of respect and the seeking of blessings through it. It is completely in line with Quranic teachings and Sharia law.

---

[140] Holy Qur'an (33:53)

7. Consideration of others

Possessing a good understanding of the blessed nature of Ziyarah should make the visitor appreciate the importance of respecting the other visitors in the shrine. This entails taking utmost care not to hurt or push anyone and trying to ensure the feelings of others are not hurt. Respect, offering smiles and kind words are important demonstrations of good moral conduct in these places. Allah mentions the need to revere the sacredness of these blessed sites by avoiding shouting or raising one's voice:

يا أَيُّهَا الَّذِينَ آمَنُوا لا تَرفَعُوا أَصواتَكُم فَوقَ صَوتِ النَّبِيِّ وَلا تَجهَرُوا لَهُ بِالقَولِ كَجَهرِ بَعضِكُم لِبَعضٍ أَن تَحبَطَ أَعمالُكُم وَأَنتُم لا تَشعُرُونَ

'O you who have faith! Do not raise your voices above the voice of the Prophet, and do not speak aloud to him as you shout to one another, lest your works should fail without you being aware.'[141]

The kissing of the *dharih* is undoubtedly good, yet the visitor must not hurt others in attempting to get reward. This is especially the case in the shrine of Imam Hussain during Arbaeen - due to the sheer volume of visitors. We must understand the Imam is displeased when we push or shove others; perhaps paying respects from afar and intending to come back later when the shrine is not as congested is the best solution.

8. Recitation of established Ziyarah

It is highly recommended to greet and send salutations upon the Prophet and his family using the supplications and invocations narrated from them. Each member of the Ahlulbayt has a designated Ziyarah or more, and there are some that can be recited for all the Ma'someen. This includes Ziyarah Ameenullah, which is amongst the most authentic ziyarahs we have.

---

[141] Holy Qur'an (49:2)

For Imam Hussain ﷺ, there are general Ziyarats and specific ones for the time of visitation. General Ziyarats include Ziyarat Ashura and Ziyarat Waritha.

After each Ziyarah, recite two rokat of Salah, known as *Salat al-Ziyarah*. For the Imams, it should be performed next to or behind the grave. Prayers, whilst the mausoleum is behind the visitor, should be avoided. There is often a supplication to be recited after each recommended Salah, which further increases blessings.

9. Performance of obligatory prayers and congregational Salah

The shrines of the Ahlulbayt ﷺ are great places of worship of the Almighty ﷻ; hence, performing wajib and congregational Salah earns significant reward and blessings. This is especially the case if the prayers are performed at their recommended time (*awaal alwaqt*). Likewise, praying *qadha* (to make up missed prayers) is also encouraged in these sites and brings more reward than their performance elsewhere (except masjid Al-Nabi and Masjid Al-Haram in Makkah, where the reward is greater).

10. Facing the Mausoleum of the Ma'soom and standing whilst reciting Ziyarah

This demonstrates respect to the one the visitor has come to visit. In addition, it is recommended to touch the *dharih* (mausoleum) of the Ma'soom if possible. It is good practice to place the right cheek followed by the left on the *dharih* and ask for *hajaat* (needs and desires). It is important that consideration for others is observed and, in trying to get close to the dharih, the visitor does not injure, hurt, or push others. This is important, since the spirit and reward of Ziyarah may otherwise be lost.

11. Recitation of Salawaat

The beautiful invocation of sending blessings and salutations upon the Holy Prophet and his pure progeny has been emphasised in the Holy Qur'an:

إِنَّ اللَّهَ وَمَلائِكَتَهُ يُصَلُّونَ عَلَى النَّبِيِّ ۚ يَا أَيُّهَا الَّذِينَ آمَنُوا صَلُّوا عَلَيْهِ وَسَلِّمُوا تَسْلِيمًا

'Indeed Allah and His angels bless the Prophet; O you who have faith! Invoke blessings on him and invoke Peace upon him in a worthy manner.'[142]

The salawat is a means of earning reward, bringing forth mercy, and placing happiness in the hearts of the Ahlulbayt. Continuous salawat earns the visitor special reward, especially in these holy sites. This is affirmed by the Ahlulbayt:

'The heaviest good deed placed on the scales on the Day of Qiyama is Salawat upon Mohammad and his household.'[143]

12. Recitation of the Holy Qur'an

It is highly recommended that the visitor engages in the recitation of the mesmerising words of Allah and gifts the reward of the recitation to the Imam or holy personality they are visiting. For example, one can recite a chapter of the Qur'an and dedicate the reward of that recitation to Imam Hussain. Sitting in proximity to the glorious shrines should also allow us to reflect upon the Holy Qur'an and its practical applications in our lives.

13. Prayers and donation for others

Whilst inside the shrine, the visitor can also contribute financially to the maintenance and development of these holy places, in addition to worthy causes, such as orphans, widows, and the needy. Furthermore, it is recommended not to forget those working in these shrines and the volunteers in our duas and other believers across the world, including those who have not been blessed with the Ziyarah yet in their lives.

14. Bidding farewell

It is suggested the visitor recites the special Ziyarah when bidding farewell to the shrine. With a heavy heart, most visitors weep when

---

[142] Holy Qur'an (33:56)
[143] Bihar Al-Anwar, vol.94, p.49, no.9

visiting the shrine for the final time before returning home to their homelands. It is therefore important to speak to the Imam and ask sincerely to be given an opportunity to return once again.

Spiritual tips for the visitation of the holy shrines

For the visitors seeking spiritual elevation and increased blessings whilst at the holy shrines, some recommendations have been presented by our scholars. They include:

1. Utilise your presence inside the shrine of the Ahlulbayt to ask for *tawba* and cleanse your soul from the evil of sins. This would need to be sincere, performed with remorse over past transgressions, but with commitment not to repeat the sins. As mentioned in Qur'an (4:64), the intercession of the Holy Prophet and Ahlulbayt is an important factor for the forgiveness of sins from Allah. Consider writing down the sins committed in the past, taking this with you to the shrine, and mentioning it quietly with a sorrowful heart, seeking penitence and release from the chastisement of hell.

2. Whilst you are in the state of connecting with the *Ma'soom*, seek further enlightenment of the soul by performing recommended prayers, such as *Salat Al-Layl* and the supererogatory daily prayers. Imam Askari establishes that performing 51 rokahs (units) daily (which includes the obligatory and recommended prayers) is one of the signs of true believers.[144]

3. The Ahlulbayt have emphasised the importance of Salat Al-Layl. A myriad of worldly benefits and rewards in the akhira have been mentioned. For example:

'You must get up for the night prayer, for verily it was the devoted practice of all righteous people before you, and verily night prayer is a means of proximity (to Allah) as well as a prevention from sin.' Prophet Mohammad [145]

---

[144] Tahdhib Al-Ahkam, vol. 6, p.52
[145] Kanz al-Ummal, no.21428

'Standing up to pray at night is conducive to the health of the body, is a source of pleasure for the Lord, exposes one to (the descent of) divine mercy, and is adherence to the moral virtues of the prophets.' Imam Ali ﷺ[146]

4. Consider giving charity during your Ziyarah, for it is highly recommended for the acceptance of the deeds and forgiveness.

   'Verily charity given at night (secretly) extinguishes the wrath of the Lord, wipes away grave sins and facilitates one's account (On the Day of Resurrection). Charity given during the day makes one's wealth thrive and increases one's lifespan.' Imam Al-Sadiq ﷺ[147]

5. Pledge a commitment with the Imam that you will make a positive change in your life. This may include stopping a prohibited act, such as watching forbidden movies or backbiting. The pledge could also entail the execution of good deeds, such as supporting orphans. Reflect on whether you will be a better person going home after Ziyarah in terms of righteousness and virtue. Seek inspiration from one aspect of the life of the Imam, such as a virtue, and draw up a plan on how to apply that element into your own life. Ask the Imam to intercede and help you achieve this and grant you another opportunity to perform the Ziyarah again.

6. Do not be afraid to express your emotions, cry, and allow yourself to be drawn into the love of the holy Ahlulbayt ﷺ. It is highly fruitful to keep the feeling of love and affection strong throughout the journey, to listen to their eulogies and grieve over how they were treated. Write down your experiences and discuss them with others. Empty your heart inside the shrine and allow space and time for reflection and contemplation towards a better spiritual life.

7. Express gratitude towards them for their tireless efforts and sacrifice that enabled pure Islam to reach us today.

---

[146] Bihar Al-Anwar, v.87, p.143, no.17
[147] Bihar Al-Anwar, v.96, p.125, no.39

Chapter 14:

Brief Commentary on Ziyarat Al-Arbaeen

It has been reported from Safwan ibn Mahran that Imam Ja'far Al-Sadiq instructed the following to be recited on Arbaeen Day:[148]

Peace be upon the intimate friend of Allah, and His beloved!

Besides being the greeting of Muslims and the word uttered by angels upon receiving the inhabitants of Paradise, saying *'salaam'* (peace) is a common expression utilised by the Ahlulbayt in Ziyarah recitations. The greeting refers to the Divine attribute of God - 'Salaam' - or in reflection of peace and security bestowed by the Almighty. When we initiate the Ziyarah with such an expression, we are also establishing the belief that the Ahlulbayt hear our greeting and respond. Saying 'Salaam' projects complete submission to the command of Allah and the teachings of the noble family. This includes one's wealth, life, and time devoted to serve the path of the Almighty as espoused by His representatives on earth.

Imam Hussain is then introduced as a *wali*, which in Arabic has several meanings, but is mainly centred on a close relationship or friendship. Such a connection is established by the Ahlulbayt with The Divine, such as the statement of Imam Ali:

'O Allah, I do not worship you due to fear of your chastisement nor desire in your paradise but see you as worthy of worship and hence I worship you.'[149]

---

[148] Wasa'il Al-Shia, vol.14, p. 487. The full Ziyarah with translation is found at the end of the book in the Appendix section.
[149] Manazil Al-Akhira, p.31

In return, Allah ﷻ loves those who give everything for His sake, and dedicate their entire lives to attain His pleasure. Undoubtedly, Imam Hussain ؑ is amongst the highest of God's beloved servants, having exercised patience to such levels that even the angels were surprised at witnessing his actions.

Peace be upon the close friend of Allah, and His confidant! Peace be upon the choicest confidant of Allah, and the son of the choicest confidant [of Allah].

'*Khalil*' is used in the holy Qur'an, referring to Prophet Ibrahim ؑ (in 4:125), and indicates an individual who has reached such a status that God considers him close to Him. This is surely because of the successful passing of so many examinations and trials in this world. When we analyse the events of the Day of Ashura, we stand in complete admiration of how Imam Hussain ؑ embraced the hardships with full conviction, submission, and steadfastness. He knew that if Allah loved a servant of His, He would subject them to difficulties and calamities.

Not only is he described as a *Khalil* but also as a *Najeeb*. The latter refers to special selection by the Almighty ﷻ from the beginning, as described in *Ziyarat Warith*:

'*I bear witness that you (Imam Hussain) was light that was placed in the loins of the righteous...*'[150]

Peace be upon Hussain, the oppressed, the martyr. Peace be upon captive of agonies, and the victim of the shed tears.

Several epithets have been recorded for Imam Hussain ؑ, including *Al-Zaki* (pure one), *Al-Sabir* (the patient one), and *Al-Wafi* (the Loyal). Here, the Imam is first described as the oppressed, since not only was he dealt with unjustly and in the worst possible way by his enemies, including being deprived of water for several days - but his family were taken as captives and paraded across cities for weeks. Throughout the sermons the Imam gave before his eventual martyrdom, he highlighted that he had not wronged anyone, usurped no property, nor was there any justification for the cruel way he was being treated. By calling him out as the oppressed, we are encouraged to be the voice of those seeking justice

---

[150] Mafatihul Jinan, p.298

against tyrants and to be actively supporting the oppressed around the world - in any capacity.

Not only was the Imam ؑ unjustly treated, but he became the Master of Martyrs, sacrificing his life for Allah and the protection of religion. He continues to be the beacon and inspiration for all freedom-seeking people and those yearning to understand the meaning of sacrifice and altruism.

Upon recognising the tragedy that befell the Imam and those with him, the reciter is then reminded of the importance of shedding tears in remembrance of the grief of Ashura. It is Imam Hussain ؑ who is reported to have said:

'I am the victim of the tears. No believer shall remember me except that their eyes will water.'[151]

This was the practice of the Holy Prophet Mohammad ﷺ, who wept often upon remembering the tragedy of his grandson, Imam Hussain ؑ. Many narrations emphasise the reward for shedding tears in this regard. Crying is also a demonstration of love and loyalty, a form of veneration towards the signs of Allah, repentance from sins and an awakening of the conscience to stand against oppression and injustice. Without doubt, the real and effective tears are those that translate to action, instilling positive change into the human being and instigating reform and progression towards righteousness.

O Allah, I do bear witness that he is verily Your intimate servant and son of Your intimate servant, Your choice and son of Your choice, and the winner of Your honouring. You have honoured him with martyrdom, endued him with happiness, privileged him with legitimate birth, made him one of the chiefs, one of the leaders, and one of the defenders (of Your religion), gave him the inheritances of the Prophets, and chose him as argument against Your created beings and one of the Prophets' successors.

The testimony is an important declaration of the belief that Imam Hussain ؑ is God's chosen representative and his obedience is obligatory upon mankind. This was the main issue on the plains of Karbala, whereby the army that stood against him chose the *wilayah* of Yazid and

---

[151] Kamil Al-Ziyarat, p.133

Bani Ummayah over the legitimate authority of the Ahlulbayt ﷺ. What follows is unrelenting belief that the actions and movement of the Imam were exactly as God wanted, whilst rejecting suggestions that he, for example, should not have risen against the tyrannical establishment or that he should have stayed in Medina. The latter is promulgated by some people, even today, arguing the Imam did not follow the advice of some, including the companions of the Prophet. In reality, the many statements of the Prophet to support Imam Hussain ﷺ categorically establish the validity of his uprising and movements:

'Hussain is from me and I am from Hussain.'[152]
'Hasan and Hussain are Imams, whether they rise or not.'[153]

Imam Sadiq ﷺ establishes in this Ziyarah how martyrdom in the way of Allah is an honour bestowed by the Almighty ﷻ upon the martyrs, which ultimately resulted in optimum happiness and satisfaction. Imam Sajjad ﷺ reaffirms this:

'Death is a norm for us, and our honour from Allah is martyrdom.'[154]

Hence, we find the first words uttered by Imam Ali ﷺ upon being struck by Abdulrahman ibn Muljim were: 'I have attained victory by the Lord of the Kaaba!'
The ultimate sweetness of the favoured intimate friends of Allah ﷻ is to meet Him, having attained His satisfaction, while knowing that anything less tantamount to a massive lost opportunity.
The affirmation of the purity of the birth of Imam Hussain ﷺ reminds mankind that those who shed his blood were born illegitimately, as narrations point out:

Imam Sadiq ﷺ is reported to have said:

'The killers of Yahya ibn Zakaria and Hussain ﷺ were born out of fornication. The heavens did not weep except for these (two).'[155]

---

[152] Musnad Ahmed ibn Hanbal, vol4, p. 172
[153] Kitab Al-Irshad, vol.2, p.30
[154] Bihar Al-Anwar, vol.45, p. 188
[155] Kamil Al-Ziyarat, p.112

Illegitimate birth is reported to be one of the characteristics of those who show enmity and hatred towards the pure progeny of the Messenger of God. The honourable lady Um Salama reports the Prophet ﷺ said to Imam Ali ؑ:

'No one hates you except that they are born illegitimately, are hypocrites or conceived whilst the mother is in menstruation.'[156]

Imam Hussain ؑ is described in this Ziyarah as a *Sayed* (chief) and a leader chosen by God. This leadership guides mankind towards perfection and righteousness and saves them from ignorance and misguidance. When asked if all the Imams are ships of salvation, it is reported that Imam Al-Ridha ؑ replied:

'Indeed we are all ships of salvation, yet the ship of Hussain is wider, and in the oceans, faster.'[157]

The Ahlulbayt ؑ are considered the teachers of mankind, without which people are at loss to discover the truth and the right path of salvation. Therefore, when the Almighty ﷻ states in the holy Qur'an: 'We shall call every nation by the leader'[158], it is the Imam of the time from the Ahlulbayt who will guide those who recognize him and follow him in this world towards eternal bliss and success in the hereafter.[159]

Anyone who studies the lives of the Ahlulbayt carefully will realise that one of their objectives was to stand against deviations and clear misconceptions about God and the religion of Islam. In this Ziyarah, the Imam ؑ affirms they also protect their followers from misguidance by praying for them, interceding with Allah, and guiding them towards the right path. Imam Hussain ؑ, alongside the other honourable Imams, is considered the inheritor of the Prophet, spreading his message of monotheism and obedience to God. Hence, we read in the famous Ziyarat Warith:

---

[156] Ilal Al-Shari. Vol.1, p.115
[157] Bihar Al-Anwar, vol.26, p.322
[158] Holy Qur'an (17:71)
[159] Al-Kafi, vol.1, p.616

'Peace be upon you, O inheritor of Adam, the chosen one of Allah;
Peace be upon you, O inheritor of Noah, the prophet of Allah;
Peace be upon you, O inheritor of Abraham, the beloved friend of Allah;
Peace be upon you, O inheritor of Moses, who received direct communication from Allah;
Peace be upon you, O inheritor of Jesus, the spirit of Allah;
Peace be upon you, O inheritor of Mohammad, the beloved friend of Allah;'[160]

The Imam inherited not only the knowledge of the Prophets, but their wisdom, mannerisms, and the righteous characteristics that make him and the Ahlulbayt legitimate leaders chosen by the Almighty. Subsequently, they are the proof of God upon all His creation - as the Ziyarah points out. The *Hujja* is the divine link, establishing the connection with the heavens, and must be on earth for existence to continue, as per the will of Allah. This is affirmed in several traditions, such as this from Imam Sadiq:

'As long as the earth is present, a proof of God must exist (on it), showing people what is permissible and what is not, whilst calling mankind towards the path of God...'[161]

Imam Ali is reported to have said:

'Verily Allah has purified and protected us (from error and sin), made us witnesses over His creation, and His proof on His earth. He made us with the Qur'an, and made the Qur'an with us, we do not leave it neither will it abandon us.'[162]

So, he called to you flawlessly, gave advices, and sacrificed his soul for you, to save Your servants from ignorance, and perplexity of straying off.

Imam Al-Sadiq affirms his grandfather, Imam Hussain, did everything possible to convince people to do the right thing and reject oppression. His eloquent sermons, pure actions, and compassionate acceptance of those who sought repentance was great proof for those

---

[160] Mafatihul Jinan, p.
[161] Basa'ir Al-Darajat, vol.10, p.527
[162] ibid, vol.2, p.114

seeking to be guided and inspired. What stood out was the sheer greatness of *akhlaq* the grandson of the Prophet displayed to give advice - never giving up hope of light entering the hearts of the thousands that surrounded him and came to fight him. His sermons on the journey to Karbala and the Day of Ashura are preserved in history as a testament to his dedication to the path.

On the Day of Ashura, Imam Hussain ﷺ addressed the army of Umar ibn Saad as follows:

'O people! Listen to my speech and do not rush till I admonish you with that which I owe you, and so that I tell you why I have come here; so, if you accept my excuse and believe my statement and fare with me with equity, you will be much happier, and you will see no reason to expose me to this. But if you do not accept my reason and do not fare with me with equity, then gather your affair and your accomplices, and do not feel sorry for what you do but effect your judgment in my regard and do not grant me any respite; surely my Lord is Allah Who revealed the Book and He looks after the righteous.

O servants of Allah! Fear Allah and be on your guard with regard to this life which, had it remained for anyone at all, the prophets would have been the worthiest of it and the most pleased with fate. But Allah created this life so that it would perish. What is new in it will soon grow old. Its pleasure diminishes and its happiness is fleeting. A man's home is but a mound, and one's house is a fort; so, get ready for the next, for the best with which you prepare yourselves is piety. Fear Allah so that you may be the winners. O people! Allah, the most Exalted One, created life and made it a temporary abode, taking its people from one condition to another. Conceited is whoever gets fascinated by it, and miserable is whoever gets infatuated by it. So, do not let this life deceive you, for it shall disappoint whoever trusts and desires it! I can see that you have all set your minds on doing something because of which you have caused Allah to curse you and to turn His Glorious Countenance away from you, causing you to be the object of His Wrath. Kind is our Lord, and mean servants of His are you! You declared obedience to and belief in Mohammad the Messenger ﷺ, then you put your ranks together to kill his Progeny and offspring! Satan took full control of you, making you forget the remembrance of Allah, the Great. Perdition, hence, is your lot and ultimate end! We belong to Allah, and to Him is our return. These are people who have turned apostates after having believed, so away with the oppressive people. O people! Identify me and find out who I am! Then go back to your evil selves and blame them, then see whether it is lawful for you to violate *my sanctity. Am I not the son of your Prophet's daughter, the son of his brother and cousin, the foremost to believe, the one who testified to the truth of what he had brought from his Lord? Is not Hamza, the Master of Martyrs, my uncle? Is not Ja'far al-Tayyar my uncle? Have you not heard that the Messenger of Allah had said about me and about my brother: "These are the masters of the youths of Paradise"? So if you believe what I say, which is the truth, let me swear by Allah that I never deliberately told a lie since I came to know that Allah hates lying and liars, and that lying is detrimental to those who invent it. But if you disbelieve in me, there are among you those who, if you ask them, can inform you of the same. Ask Jabir ibn `Abdullah al-Ansari, Abu Sa`id al-Khudari, Sahl ibn Sa'd al-S`idi, Zayd ibn Arqam, and Anas ibn Malik, and they will tell you that they have heard these hadiths of the Messenger of Allah with regard to myself and to my brother. Is this not sufficient to curb you from shedding my blood?!'*[163]

The main objective of the divinely chosen servants of God is for guidance of mankind; hence, they demonstrated total focus and loyalty for this lofty cause. The state of the society at the time of the uprising of Imam Hussain was such that hypocrisy, deception, and weakening of faith was rife. Without rising to the challenge, these vices and widespread misguidance would have been established by Bani Ummayah, and the teachings of the pure religion of Islam would have surely been distorted. Hence, Imam Hussain famously said:

'O people! The Messenger of Allah has said, "If one sees an oppressive ruler, who makes lawful what Allah has made unlawful, and he does not get him to alter his conduct through something he does or says, it will be incumbent upon Allah to resurrect him in that ruler's company. These folks have upheld Satan and abandoned their obedience to the most Merciful One, demonstrating corruption and making mischief evident.'[164]

Yet, those whom were seduced by this worldly life, who sold their share (of reward) with the lowliest and meanest, retailed their Hereafter with the cheapest price, acted haughtily, perished because of following their desires, brought to themselves Your wrath and the wrath of Your Prophet, and obeyed the dissident and hypocritical servants of You, and the bearers of the burdens (of sins) who deserve Hellfire – all those supported each other against him.

---

[163] Maqtal Al-Muqarram, p.181-182
[164] ibid, p.146

The battle of Karbala demonstrated the confrontation between the people of this world against those seeking the hereafter; the individuals who drowned in their love of materialism versus those who were intoxicated with the love of Allah ﷻ. The caravan of Imam Hussain ؏ were the latter, displaying their allegiance to the teachings of the Qur'an:

وَذَرِ الَّذِينَ اتَّخَذُوا دِينَهُمْ لَعِبًا وَلَهْوًا وَغَرَّتْهُمُ الْحَيَاةُ الدُّنْيَا ۚ وَذَكِّرْ بِهِ أَنْ تُبْسَلَ نَفْسٌ بِمَا كَسَبَتْ لَيْسَ لَهَا مِنْ دُونِ اللَّهِ وَلِيٌّ وَلَا شَفِيعٌ وَإِنْ تَعْدِلْ كُلَّ عَدْلٍ لَا يُؤْخَذْ مِنْهَا ۗ أُولَٰئِكَ الَّذِينَ أُبْسِلُوا بِمَا كَسَبُوا ۖ لَهُمْ شَرَابٌ مِنْ حَمِيمٍ وَعَذَابٌ أَلِيمٌ بِمَا كَانُوا يَكْفُرُونَ

'Leave alone those who take their religion for play and diversion and whom the life of this world has deceived, and admonish with it, lest any soul should perish because of what it has earned: It shall not have any guardian besides Allah, nor any intercessor; and though it should offer every kind of ransom, it shall not be accepted from it. They are the ones who perish because of what they have earned; they shall have boiling water for drink and a painful punishment because of what they used to defy.'[165]

Imam Hussain ؏ diagnosed the problem many people were facing because materialism had overpowered them so much that it became their god, objective, and main purpose of life:

'People are slaves of this world, and religion is just on the tongues, they turned to it whenever its suits them. Once they are hit with calamities, the religious ones are very few.'[166]

The epic of Karbala gave us several such individuals, who missed a great opportunity to embrace the path of martyrdom, but instead, continued the way of Satan and ultimately deep remorse. One such person was Ubaydillah ibn Al-Hur, who was visited by Imam Hussain ؏ on the way to Karbala, invited to join the army of truth. Ubaydillah declined, citing the need to stay with his family and protect his wealth!

As Imam Sadiq ؏ has reportedly mentioned in this Ziyarah, such individuals sold their afterlife cheaply and never enjoyed their worldly gains either. Such an unfortunate individual was Umar ibn Sa'ad, who knew the position of Imam Hussain ؏ and his noble status, yet was

---

[165] Holy Qur'an (6:70)
[166] Tuhaf Al-Uqool, p.174

deceived by the desire to be the Governor of the town of Rey (modern day Tehran, Iran). He decided to fight the Imam, despite all the warnings, and yet never attained his worldly wishes. Imam Ali beautifully summarises such a fate:

'Whomsoever sells his world for akhira will attain them both, but whoever sells their hereafter for this world will lose them both.'[167]

The Imam then identifies a major reason people choose the wrong option and sell their hereafter for this world: arrogance and the love of desire (*Hawa*). These two vices are the most devastating that can affect human beings, with disastrous consequences in both worlds. The Qur'an affirms that some consider their desire as their god, obeying it at every opportunity and stopping at nothing to fulfil its pleasure:

أَفَرَأَيْتَ مَنِ اتَّخَذَ إِلَٰهَهُ هَوَاهُ

'Have you seen him who has taken his desire to be his god...'[168]

In a narration, Imam Ali warns of the consequences of taking our desires as the object of worship and obeying them uncontrollably:

'I fear for you two things; the following of desire and prolonged (false) hope. As for following desires, for it becomes a barrier to the truth, and the prolonging of (false) hope makes one forget the hereafter.'[169]

Subsequently, the evil actions of the people brought about the anger of the Prophet and the Ahlulbayt and therefore the wrath of Allah. As Imam Hussain famously said, the pleasure of Allah is directly connected to the happiness of His chosen servants, the Ahlulbayt:

'The pleasure of Allah is the pleasure of us the Ahlulbayt, for we are patient with His Decree, and He rewards us with reward of the patient ones.'[170]

---

[167] Ghurar Al-Hikam, p.147
[168] Holy Qur'an (45:23)
[169] Al-Kafi, vol.2, p.323
[170] Al-Luhuf, p.25

By perpetrating one of the worst crimes in the history of mankind, those that participated in shedding the blood of Imam Hussain, his family, and noble companions have undoubtedly carried a huge burden of transgression and sin, for which the chastisement of Allah awaits in the hereafter. The majority were disgraced and humiliated in this world first, when the likes of Mukhtar Al-Thaqafi captured and bought them to justice. Similarly, they will face the justice of Allah in this world when many will return at the *Rajah*[171] and will be humiliated once again.

The Qur'an informs us of the severe repercussions of the deliberate killing of a believer, let alone the grandson of the Prophet and noble people around him:

وَمَنْ يَقْتُلْ مُؤْمِنًا مُتَعَمِّدًا فَجَزَاؤُهُ جَهَنَّمُ خَالِدًا فِيهَا وَغَضِبَ اللَّهُ عَلَيْهِ وَلَعَنَهُ وَأَعَدَّ لَهُ عَذَابًا عَظِيمًا

'Should anyone kill a believer intentionally, his requital shall be hell, to remain in it [forever]; Allah shall be wrathful at him and curse him and He shall prepare for him a great punishment.'[172]

However, he fought against them painstakingly with steadfastness expecting Your reward. until his blood was shed on account of his obedience to You, and his women were violated.

There was no hesitation on the part of Imam Hussain ﷺ for calling Jihad against the tyrannical rule of Yazid and Bani Ummayah. Despite the fears and constant assassination attempts, his patience shone all the way through, whilst knowing he would be brutally butchered and his family taken as a cruel form of victor's justice. The Ziyarah outlines that the reason for hatred towards the Imam and his message was pure obedience to Allah ﷻ and the rejection of submission towards the impure and tyrannical rule of Yazid. This resulted not only in the massacre of the Imam and the majority of his companions, but the enslavement and parading of his family across Kufa and Damascus. They were tortured, mocked, threatened to be sold off, laughed at, and mocked, whilst hijabs were snatched from the women.

The fact that all the Imam's actions were for the sake of the Almighty ﷻ highlights an important message for us all; the path of God is not

---

[171] This is the belief, exclusive to the Shia, that Allah will bring back in this world the best and worst of His creation to establish His Justice before the day of judgment
[172] Holy Qur'an (4:93)

necessarily easy and will be filled with hardships and trials. Shaitan will do his utmost to derail the believer from the straight path by planting and presenting many obstacles, temptations, and people as barriers in this journey. Yet, the inspirational story of Ashura teaches mankind that, by aligning oneself with Allah, eternal victory is undoubtedly achieved. Yazid and his cronies have been cursed for centuries, whilst the remembrance of the grandson of the Prophet lives on and intensifies. Whatever is done for God is enhanced by Him.

So, O Allah, pour heavy curses on them, and chastise them with painful chastisement.

The withdrawal of the mercy of Allah is among the strongest punishments inflicted upon human beings. *La'an* has been referred to 33 times in the Qur'an in various chapters, described as a result of some actions of humans. For example:

إِنَّ الَّذِينَ يُؤْذُونَ اللَّهَ وَرَسُولَهُ لَعَنَهُمُ اللَّهُ فِي الدُّنْيَا وَالْآخِرَةِ وَأَعَدَّ لَهُمْ عَذَابًا مُهِينًا

'Indeed those who torment Allah and His Apostle are cursed by Allah in the world and the Hereafter, and He has prepared a humiliating punishment for them.'[173]

What is a worse way to incur the wrath of Allah ﷻ and His Messenger other than the slaughter of the grandson of the Prophet and his followers, deprive them of water, torture his family, and take them as captives? Therefore, we find the concept of *la'an* used in many supplications and Ziyarah recitations, and it's a demonstration of the rejection of falsehood and the distancing from the enemies of God. The more *la'an* is uttered against them, the more and worse punishment they receive from the Almighty - which is fully deserved.

Peace be upon you, O son of Allah's Messenger. Peace be upon you, O son of the chief of the Prophets' successors. I bear witness that you are verily the trustee of Allah and the son of His trustee.

---

[173] Holy Qur'an (33:57)

The fact that Imam Hussain ؑ is one of the grandsons of the Prophet Mohammad ﷺ is established in the Qur'an, when referring to the famous incident of *Mubahala*:

فَمَنْ حَاجَّكَ فِيهِ مِن بَعْدِ مَا جَاءَكَ مِنَ الْعِلْمِ فَقُلْ تَعَالَوْا نَدْعُ أَبْنَاءَنَا وَأَبْنَاءَكُمْ وَنِسَاءَنَا وَنِسَاءَكُمْ وَأَنفُسَنَا وَأَنفُسَكُمْ ثُمَّ نَبْتَهِلْ فَنَجْعَل لَّعْنَتَ اللَّهِ عَلَى الْكَاذِبِينَ

'Should anyone argue with you concerning him, after the knowledge that has come to you, say, 'Come! Let us call our sons and your sons, our women and your women, our souls and your souls, then let us pray earnestly and call down Allah's curse upon the liars.'[174]

It is agreed by most scholars across Muslim schools that the sons referred to in the verse are Imams Hasan ؑ and Hussain ؑ, who were joined by the Prophet, Imam Ali, and lady Fatima ؑ in the malediction process with the Christians of Najran (outside Medina).

Unfortunately, the fact that Imam Hussain ؑ was the grandson of the Prophet as well as the son of Imam Ali and the Lady of Light did not make those individuals involved in the tragedy of Karbala stop the massacre or think twice before shedding his blood. The Imam reminded them of this on numerous occasions, lest they claim later that they were deceived to believe it was a different person.

Imam Sadiq ؑ describes his grandfather as a trustee of God, who was entrusted to protect the faith from distortion and fabrication. The objective of Yazid and the Umayyad clan was to return the people to the time of ignorance and polytheism. Yazid could not hide his rejection of Islam when he recited lines of poetry whilst poking the blessed head of Imam Hussain:

'I wish my forefathers at Badr had witnessed
How the Khazraj are by the thorns annoyed,
They would have Glorified and Unified Allah
Then they would make *tahlil* and say in elation:
May your hands, O Yazid, never be paralyzed![175]

---

[174] Holt Qur'an (3:61)
[175] Maqtal Al-Muqarram, p. 297

From the outset, Imam Hussain refused to give allegiance to Yazid, highlighting the dangerous future the Islamic ummah would face if he continued to be in power:

'We are the household of the Prophet, the substance of the Message, the ones visited by the angels; it is through us that Allah initiates and concludes. Yazid is a man of sin, a drunkard, a murderer of the soul the killing of which Allah has prohibited, a man who is openly promiscuous. A man like me shall never swear the oath of allegiance to a man like him.'[176]

You lived with happiness, passed away with praiseworthiness, and died missed, wronged, and martyred.

The hallmarks of the true and intimate friends of the Almighty are that, despite all the hardship they endure in this world, they live with happiness and tranquillity. This is because they have understood this life is transient and short, therefore cannot be compared with the hereafter and the eternal bliss of Allah. Therefore, they know that whatever they are subjected to is to raise their status in the real (after) life:

وَمَا هَٰذِهِ الْحَيَاةُ الدُّنْيَا إِلَّا لَهْوٌ وَلَعِبٌ ۚ وَإِنَّ الدَّارَ الْآخِرَةَ لَهِيَ الْحَيَوَانُ ۚ لَوْ كَانُوا يَعْلَمُونَ

'The life of this world is nothing but diversion and play, but the abode of the Hereafter is indeed Life, had they known!'[177]

True happiness is the correct preparation for eternal joy and satisfaction. It is undoubtedly achieved through the correct following of God's chosen servants, as we read in the famous Ziyarah *Al-Jamia Al-Kabeera*:

'Happy are those who follow you (o Ahlulbayt), and lost are those who oppose you...'[178]

The Qur'an, being the constitution of well-being, emphatically establishes that true and real happiness lies in wait for the believers who submit entirely to God's generative and legislative will and are patient

---

[176] ibid, p.29
[177] Holy Qur'an (29:64)
[178] Mafatihul Jinan, p. 355

whilst obedient to Him. Therefore, narrations tell us that, despite what Imam Hussain ﷺ endured on Ashura, his face was beaming with light, and he never broke down or gave up. The Ziyarah then expresses how the happiness that was part of the life of the Imam resulted in him attaining praise from Allah ﷻ, whereby his remembrance is echoed continuously across the world. The unceasing legacy of the Master of Martyrs is an important lesson for mankind that the Almighty ﷻ will elevate the remembrance of those who give everything for Him and for His cause.

I also bear witness that Allah shall inevitably fulfil His promise to You, exterminate those who disappointed you, and chastise those who slew you.

One cannot doubt the promise of the Almighty ﷻ, which is found in the Qur'an in numerous places:

وَعَدَ اللَّهُ الَّذِينَ آمَنُوا مِنكُمْ وَعَمِلُوا الصَّالِحَاتِ لَيَسْتَخْلِفَنَّهُمْ فِي الْأَرْضِ كَمَا اسْتَخْلَفَ الَّذِينَ مِن قَبْلِهِمْ وَلَيُمَكِّنَنَّ لَهُمْ دِينَهُمُ الَّذِي ارْتَضَىٰ لَهُمْ وَلَيُبَدِّلَنَّهُم مِّن بَعْدِ خَوْفِهِمْ أَمْنًا ۚ يَعْبُدُونَنِي لَا يُشْرِكُونَ بِي شَيْئًا

'*Allah has promised those of you who have faith and do righteous deeds that He will surely make them successors in the earth, just as He made those who were before them successors, and He will surely establish for them their religion which He has approved for them, and that He will surely change their state to security after their fear, while they worship Me, not ascribing any partners to Me...*'[179]

The sacrifice of the Imam ﷺ, alongside his family and companions, was an important step for the fulfilment of the promise of God, which will eventually be fulfilled after the reappearance of the grandson of Imam Hussain, the awaited saviour, Imam Al-Mahdi ﷺ. Thereafter, according to the numerous verses and traditions of the Ahlulbayt ﷺ, the best and the worst of God's creation will be brought back to life during the *Rajah* to witness the justice of God administered here on this earth before the Day of Judgement. Undoubtedly, one of those who will return is Imam Hussain ﷺ and diametrically the likes of Yazid. The realisation of the following will then be witnessed:

---

[179] Holy Qur'an (24:55)

إِنَّا لَنَنصُرُ رُسُلَنَا وَالَّذِينَ آمَنُوا فِي الْحَيَاةِ الدُّنْيَا وَيَوْمَ يَقُومُ الْأَشْهَادُ

'Indeed We shall grant victory to Our apostles and those who have faith in the life of the world and on the day when the witnesses rise up.'[180]

I also bear witness that you fulfilled your pledge to Allah, and strove hard in His way until death came upon you.

Imam Hussain ﷺ is the champion of *tawhid* (monotheism) and died defending it. This is the fulfilment of the pledge that the Almighty ﷻ took from every human before this world:

وَإِذْ أَخَذَ رَبُّكَ مِن بَنِي آدَمَ مِن ظُهُورِهِمْ ذُرِّيَّتَهُمْ وَأَشْهَدَهُمْ عَلَىٰ أَنفُسِهِمْ أَلَسْتُ بِرَبِّكُمْ ۖ قَالُوا بَلَىٰ ۛ شَهِدْنَا ۛ أَن تَقُولُوا يَوْمَ الْقِيَامَةِ إِنَّا كُنَّا عَنْ هَٰذَا غَافِلِينَ

'When your Lord took from the Children of Adam, from their loins, their descendants and made them bear witness over themselves, [He said to them,] 'Am I not your Lord?' They said, 'Yes indeed! We bear witness.' [This,] lest you should say on the Day of Resurrection, 'Indeed we were unaware of this.''[181]

What is clear is the need to struggle throughout our lives to keep this promise alive, since Satan and his army work continuously to derail the human from this noble objective. The inspirational personality of Imam Hussain ﷺ was such that those around him were inspired by some of his qualities, such as loyalty. He was the teacher, who not only spread his knowledge but acted by example.

The word used to refer to death here is *yaqeen* (certainty), since it is derived from the following Qur'anic verse:

وَاعْبُدْ رَبَّكَ حَتَّىٰ يَأْتِيَكَ الْيَقِينُ

'And worship your Lord until death comes to you.'[182]

---

[180] Holy Qur'an (40:51)
[181] Holy Qur'an (7:172)
[182] Holt Qur'an (15:99)

After death, every human being will attain certainty and cannot deny God or reject Him.

So, may Allah curse those who slew you. May Allah curse those who wronged you. May Allah curse the people who, when informed about that, were pleased with it.

The three groups of people deserving the withdrawal of the mercy of Allah ﷻ as presented here are those who shed the blood of the Imam, those who assisted in this objective, and the people who became complicit by displaying pleasure when hearing of the atrocity. The religion of Islam propagates the importance of enjoining good and forbidding evil, and simply standing on the fence in the face of oppression and wrongdoing is akin to tacit approval for the action. Today, the call is also relevant, since we witness oppression and injustice being perpetrated in different degrees around the world. Staying silent without voicing our condemnation nor actively working to help the oppressed will bring about punishment from the Almighty ﷻ. The revolutionary spirit of Imam Hussain ؏ should live on in our thoughts and actions and should inspire us to do whatever we can to stand against injustice anywhere, starting with ourselves and our families.

A widespread problem at the time of the tragedy of Karbala was apathy and a lack of willingness to instigate fruitful change to stand with the truth. The blood of the martyrs of Karbala ignited the passion amongst many, including the penitents and others, to seek social justice and to sacrifice their lives for this noble cause. The eternal words of Imam Hussain ؏ in rejecting oppression should reverberate at all times, reminding us of our responsibilities and the dangerous repercussions of remaining indifferent.

O Allah, I do ask You to witness for me that I am loyal to those who are loyal to him, and enemy of those who are enemies of him.

The belief in the importance of loving the Ahlulbayt ؏ and rejecting their enemies constitutes part of the *Furoo al-deen* (branches of Islam), according to the Shia school of thought. The love of the Ahlulbayt and the love of their enemies cannot co-exist in the heart of a believer. This is because the Almighty ﷻ has stipulated in the Qur'an that He has created no one with two hearts.[183] The one heart we have is unidirectional - in that righteousness and falsehood cannot be combined. If they somehow are, the fruits of following the truth are nullified and not obtained.

Hence, the concept of *wilayah* and *bara'a* are integral to keep the believer within the path that God has ordained upon those seeking salvation, not that of Satan.

May my father and mother be accepted as ransoms for you, O son of Allah's Messenger. I bear witness that you were light in the sublime loins, and purified wombs; the impurities of the Ignorance Era could not object you to filth, nor could its murky clothes dress you.

A demonstration of intense love and respect is exhibited when a person offers their father and mother as sacrifice for another. This is a well-known expression within the Arab world. The intense love that billions have had throughout history for Imam Hussain ﷺ is not coincidental, but stems from the Divine grace he received after giving all for the Almighty. It can be said that Hussain gave his heart to Allah, and Allah gave the hearts of humanity to Hussain!

The testimony that follows establishes the belief that the Ahlulbayt are illuminating lights created by Allah ﷻ that passed through the loins of honourable and pure mothers and fathers, who never bowed to idols and were entirely monotheistic. This belief is rooted in many narrations of the Ahlulbayt. Honourable individuals, such as Abdul-Mutalib, Abu Talib, Abdullah, and Fatima bint Asad, all worshipped Allah alone and never accepted or practiced polytheism.

وَجَعَلَهَا كَلِمَةً بَاقِيَةً فِي عَقِبِهِ لَعَلَّهُمْ يَرْجِعُونَ

'And He made it a lasting word among his posterity so that they may come back [to the right path].'[184]

This is referring to *tawhid* (monotheism), meaning from the loins of Ibrahim, it continued to be passed on from one generation to another.

---

[183] Holy Qur'an (33:4)
[184] Holy Qur'an (43:28)

I also bear witness that you are one of the mainstays of the religion, the supports of Muslims, and the haven of the believers

A building cannot stand without the walls and pillars. It is supported by these structures. Imam Hussain is described as the pillar and support for Islam and Muslims. This applies to all the Ahlulbayt, whose love and following constitute the mainstay and foundation of the religion of Islam:

'Everything has a foundation, and the foundation of Islam is the love of us the Ahlulbayt.'[185]

Sayida Fatima reaffirms this in her famous sermon, where she states:

'...the obligation to obey us (the Ahlul Bayt) has been prescribed to set up order in the community, and our authority (imamah) has been prescribed to save the people from differences.'[186]

In particular, Imam Hussain is also a haven for believers, for he is presented by the Prophet as the lantern of guidance and the ship of salvation. Those who embark on the ship of Hussain will feel the protection from the tides of ignorance and deviation.

I also bear witness that you are the God-fearing, righteous, pleased, immaculate, guide, and well-guided Imam.

The seven qualities of the Imam outlined in the Ziyarah are commonly found in other ziyarahs as well. These characteristics and more made the Imams of the Ahlulbayt a magnet for those seeking the truth and wanting to discover the path of the Almighty. It also highlights to people the need to inculcate as many of these virtues into our lives as possible. If a believer wants to be a true follower of Imam Hussain, then much effort must be exerted to reflect these attributes in our lives and make them our second nature. The more pious, pleased

---

[185] Bihar Al-Anwar, vol. 74, p.158
[186] Al-Ihtijaj, vol.1, p.258

with God's will, and righteous we become, the closer position we attain with the Imam ؑ and ultimately with our Creator.

Consider how Imam Hussain ؑ taught an individual who asked him how to stop committing sins. He told him that if he could fulfil any of the following five conditions, then he could sin as much as he likes. First, to go anywhere that God cannot see him. Second, to find a place where God is not in charge. Third, to eat from that which God did not create. Fourth, to delay the angel of death from taking the soul. The fifth is to deny the angel of hell from taking the individual towards hellfire.[187]

While cleverly instilling the point that it is impossible to hide from God, we can see how the Imams would adopt different methods to awaken the conscience of people. Appreciating and implementing their guidance helps people understand how to strengthen their *nafs* and gain *taqwa*.

And I bear witness that the Imams from your progeny are the spokesmen of piety, the signs of guidance, the firmest handle (of Islam), and the decisive Argument against the inhabitants of the world.

Narrations tell us that Imam Hussain ؑ was favoured in that the soil of his grave is a means of healing, the dua in his shrine is answered by Allah ﷻ, and the Imams of the Ahlulbayt ؑ are from his progeny.[188]

The honourable Imams are described as the *Kalimat Al-Taqwa* because they are the teachers through which people understand *Taqwa* (God consciousness) and the words of Allah ﷻ, the Qur'an. In addition, the belief in them and their following is an important pre-requisite for the acceptance of deeds by Allah ﷻ. They are described as the *Urwat al-Wuthqa* (firmest bond), since they are the rope to hold on to for salvation and well-being.

I also bear witness that I believe in you all and in your Return, I have full confidence in the laws of my religion and in the seals of my deeds, my heart is at peace with you all, all my affairs are based on your commands, and my support for you all is already all set, until Allah permits you.

---

[187] Bihar Al-Anwar, vol.75, p.126
[188] A'mali Al-Tusi, vol.1, p.324

Over 200 narrations discuss the return or the *Rajah* of the righteous and the most wretched servants of God before the Day of Resurrection in this world. It is an important belief within the school of Ahlulbayt ﷺ. Despite disagreement on the details of the *Rajah*, the concept is considered authentic, and the belief in it essential as part of the Shia teachings. The philosophy of such a return is not necessarily vengeance but the demonstration of the might of God in administering justice witnessed by His best creation against the worst of mankind.

The Imam then affirms the importance of demonstrating the love of Imam Hussain ﷺ through adherence to Sharia teachings, the latter being reflected in actions. Imam Baqir ﷺ once informed Jabir:

'Does it suffice for one who claims to be our follower to just express his friendship with the members of the Holy Household? I swear by God that no one is our true follower unless he fears God and obeys Him. Our followers are known for their humbleness and frequent remembrance of God; fasting; praying; helping the orphans, the needy, the ones in debt, and needy neighbours; reading the Quran; and talking properly with the people. They have always been trustworthy in their tribes. O' Jabir! Do not let the various sects affect you. Do you think that it suffices for one to say that he likes Imam Ali and he is his follower, but does not do anything to support his claim? Or he says that he likes the Prophet, who is even better than Imam Ali, but does not take his example and follow his deeds and act according to the Prophet's tradition? Just having love for the Prophet is of no use for him. Therefore, fear God, and act in such a way as to attain what is near God, since there is no relation of kin between God and anyone. The one most loved by God is the one who is the most pious, and the noblest one is the one who fears God and obeys Him. I swear by God that it is not possible to get close to God unless by His obedience, and we do not hold the key to relief from the Fire of Hell, and no one has any authority over God. Whoever is obedient to God is our friend, and whoever disobeys God is our enemy. No one can attain our friendship unless by having nobility and piety.'[189]

So, I am with you. I am with you, not with your enemies.

Therefore, as we believe in them (both through our heart and actions) and their return, we will instead commit to remaining submissive in our

---

[189] Al-Kafi, vol.2, p.80

hearts and obedient to their command, refusing to abandon them and their teachings. At the same time, the danger of adhering to their enemies is highlighted, and a promise is made not to side with those who sought to stand against them. This part of Ziyarah reiterates the concepts of *wilayah* and *bara'a*.

Allah's blessings be upon you, upon your souls, upon your bodies, upon the present and the absent from you, and upon the apparent and the invisible from you. Respond to us, O Lord of the Worlds.

Finally, the choicest and best salutations of God are sent upon their blessed and pure souls and bodies, including the awaited saviour, who is present, yet invisible, from human beings.

Chapter 15:

The Meaning of Labbayk Ya Hussain

*L*abbayk Ya Hussain. A chant uttered by millions as they walk to Karbala. What does it mean?

The following is a summary of a lecture I delivered on this subject during Muharram 2016:

One of the most uttered sentences by hundreds of millions across the world in the commemoration of the martyrdom of Imam Hussain ؈ is *Labbayk Ya Hussain*. Men, women, children, and the elderly from different backgrounds and corners of the world feel a great sense of passion when uttering these words. This includes non-Arabic speakers, such as people from Thailand, Ghana, Singapore, and Brazil!

Meaning 'I am responding to your call oh Hussain', the millions who chant this respond to the rallying call of Imam Hussain ؈ made on the Day of Ashura: 'Is there anyone to help us?' Undoubtedly, the continuous utterance of this and other chants is the demonstration of the deep love and connection that people have had, for hundreds of years, with the grandson of the Prophet. *Labbayk Ya Hussain* has been chanted by people at times of attack or difficulty; for example, after explosions went off in places, like Baghdad or Pakistan, people reacted by calling out enthusiastically and reaffirming their allegiance to the Imam.

The first question to ask is: Is such a statement permissible in Islam? Some have suggested it constitutes polytheism, since it involves calling out to people who have died, and *Labbayk* is only uttered to God (as in Hajj and umrah during the process of *ihram*).

In response, Arabic lexicographers and experts point out that '*Labbayk*' means:

a) 'I continue on your obedience'
b) 'I respond to your invitation any time'

It is a common expression utilised by the Arabs, whereby people use it to respond to someone deemed to be in a position of authority. There is no evidence of its restrictive usage in the *talbiya* in hajj, as we are demonstrating our response to Allah's invitation to perform the hajj rituals and therefore submit to Him.

The Holy Qur'an also affirms those slayed in the path of Allah ﷻ are alive:

وَلَا تَحْسَبَنَّ الَّذِينَ قُتِلُوا فِي سَبِيلِ اللَّهِ أَمْوَاتًا ۚ بَلْ أَحْيَاءٌ عِندَ رَبِّهِمْ يُرْزَقُونَ

'Do not suppose those who were slain in the way of Allah to be dead; rather they are living and provided for near their Lord.'[190]

To respond to the call of an individual calling to Allah ﷻ is also deemed necessary:

يَا قَوْمَنَا أَجِيبُوا دَاعِيَ اللَّهِ وَآمِنُوا بِهِ

'O our people! Respond to Allah's summoner and have faith in Him.'[191]

Books of narrations also point out that the companions used to respond to Prophet Mohammad ﷺ by saying: 'Labbayk'.[192]

With regards to the calling of the name, the Prophet used to call for Imam Ali ؑ for example by saying 'Ya Ali' in numerous occasions. Given that the Qur'an tells us that these holy personalities are alive, calling them is totally acceptable.

An important consideration to ask thereafter is, what does this statement mean, and what should we have in our minds when we utter these words?

Relationship with Allah ﷻ

This is the most important relationship we should develop, and we should constantly reflect on our relationship with our Creator? What affects it? How can we improve it?

---

[190] Holy Qur'an (3:169)
[191] Holy Qur'an (46:31)
[192] Sahih Bukhari, vol. 6, p.196

The first consideration is whether we are pleased with God. Imam Ali beautifully presents how we should reflect this into our lives:

'Oh my Lord, it's a matter of dignity that I am your servant, and it's a matter of pride that You are my Lord. You are exactly how I want you to be, so make me how You want me to be.'[193]

But how can we prove we are pleased with the Almighty?

Demonstrating submission and steadfastness associated with the generative and legislative answer is the key. The generative will of God is what He has decreed upon the universe, such as the system of trials and tribulations that every human will invariably face. The legislative will of God is what He has commanded us to perform and other things to stay away from.

Therefore, the Almighty may take away some things from us, such as health, wealth, and security for example. Unfortunately, some people may go through depression, anxiety, psycho-sematic disorders, and need medications. For the believers, the best anti-depressant is the remembrance of Allah and reliance on Him, knowing fully well that He is in control of everything and knows what is happening to us. That is why the honourable Lady of Patience, Sayida Zainab, famously responded to the question of the tyrant on her view of events by saying:

'I have not seen anything but beauty.'[194]

When we utter *Labbayk Ya Hussain*, we are emphasising our commitment and loyalty to our connection with Allah, since to get closer to Allah, we need to get closer to Hussain, and to get closer to Hussain would lead us closer to Allah. That is why Imam Hussain invited people to free themselves from the shackles of enslavement to this world and materialism, and attach themselves instead to the mercy and blessings of God.

---

[193] Bihar Al-Anwar, vol.2, p.88
[194] Maqtal Al-Muqarram, p. 277

The Problem of Apathy and Hypocrisy

We can also understand this statement by looking at the situation of the society at that time and the debilitating spiritual illness that was widespread. One aspect was the distinct lack of will to instigate change or to stand up for the truth. Examples of the people of Kufa and some members of Bani Asad, who were approached by the companion of the Imam Habib ibn Mudhahir, come to mind. Some of the tribe refused to assist and preferred to stay away.

Unfortunately, people had created a mask of illusion and were infatuated with desires that weakened their resolve and made them reluctant to side with the truth. They ignored important matters, trivialised faith, were seeking to fit in, and became overpowered by false promises. They preferred to 'sit on the fence' and observe what was happening, fearful of the outcome upon their families or businesses if they sided with the grandson of the Prophet.

When we stand and passionately cry out *Labbayk Ya Hussain*, we should be wary not to fall into the same trap as many during the time of the Imam who did not support him. We should be active members of society, serving at many levels, seeking to help the oppressed and the needy.

Today, we live in a world spread with bigotry, violence, and disunity. When we stand to answer the call of the Imam, our goal should be to foster an environment of peace and harmony, championing common human values of respect and kindness. We should re-iterate the famous call of Imam Ali:

'People are of two kinds: either your brother in faith or equal in humanity.'[195]

---

[195] Nahjul Balagha, Letter 53

Labbayk Ya Hussain means to work to establish honesty, integrity, sincerity, truthfulness, sacrifice, strong ethical traits, equity, justice, human rights, dignity, and other human values wherever we are.

Labbayk Ya Hussain entails us being brave and courageous against oppressors and tyrants, seeking justice even if it means sacrificing our lives.

Labbayk Ya Hussain is a demonstration of loyalty towards the awaited saviour Imam Mehdi ﷼ that we will work to build the foundation for his reappearance by positively improving ourselves and building a strong community.

Labbayk Ya Hussain is a call for reform and progression, in line with what Sharia law instructs and directs, to make sure we are not stagnant nor do we transgress into innovations or distortions.

Labbayk Ya Hussain is a call to examine our conduct with others and the way we deal with people in society, in line with the Qur'an and the teachings of Ahlulbayt ﷼.

Labbayk Ya Hussain is affirmation of our love and loyalty towards the pure progeny of the Prophet ﷺ and that we continue to follow them, remember their various occasions, and uphold their principles and teachings, at whatever cost.

Labbayk Ya Hussain is commitment to continue the sessions of mourning, azaa, remembrance of Ashura, and the walk of the Arbaeen as long as we are alive, and to encourage others to participate as well.

Labayk Ya Hussain is the expression of love and submission to Allah ﷻ, and to those who gave their lives in the path of Allah ﷻ.

السَّلامُ عليْك يا ابا عبْد الله وعلى الأرْواح الَّتي حلَّتْ بفنائك عليْك منّي سلامُ الله ابدا ما بقيتُ وبقي اللَّيْلُ والنَّهارُ ولا جعلهُ الله آخر الْعهْد منّي لزيارتكُمْ، السَّلامُ على الْحُسيْن وعلى عليِّ بْن الْحُسيْن وعلى اوْلاد الْحُسيْن وعلى اصْحاب الْحُسيْن

Peace be on you, O Abu Abdullah, and on those souls who came to your camp to put themselves at your disposal.

As long as I am alive and the days and nights follow each other, I invoke Allah to send blessings on you forever and ever.

May Allah not make this pledge of close association, physical and spiritual, with you the last fulfilment.

Peace be on Hussain, and on Ali son of Hussain, and on the children of Hussain, and on the friends of Hussain.

Appendix

Ziyarat Arbaeen

اَلسَّلَامُ عَلَى وَلِيِّ اللهِ وَ حَبِيبِهِ ، اَلسَّلَامُ عَلَى خَلِيلِ اللهِ وَ نَجِيبِهِ ، اَلسَّلَامُ عَلَى صَفِيِّ اللهِ وَ ابْنِ صَفِيِّهِ ، اَلسَّلَامُ عَلَى الْحُسَيْنِ الْمَظْلُومِ الشَّهِيدِ ، اَلسَّلَامُ عَلَى أَسِيرِ الْكُرُبَاتِ وَ قَتِيلِ الْعَبَرَاتِ

اَللَّهُمَّ إِنِّي أَشْهَدُ أَنَّهُ وَلِيُّكَ وَ ابْنُ وَلِيِّكَ ، وَ صَفِيُّكَ وَ ابْنُ صَفِيِّكَ ، الْفَائِزُ بِكَرَامَتِكَ ، أَكْرَمْتَهُ بِالشَّهَادَةِ ، وَ حَبَوْتَهُ بِالسَّعَادَةِ ، وَ اجْتَبَيْتَهُ بِطِيبِ الْوِلَادَةِ ، وَ جَعَلْتَهُ سَيِّداً مِنَ السَّادَةِ ، وَ قَائِداً مِنَ الْقَادَةِ ، وَ ذَائِداً مِنَ الذَّادَةِ ، وَ أَعْطَيْتَهُ مَوَارِيثَ الْأَنْبِيَاءِ ، وَ جَعَلْتَهُ حُجَّةً عَلَى خَلْقِكَ مِنَ الْأَوْصِيَاءِ ، فَأَعْذَرَ فِي الدُّعَاءِ ، وَ مَنَحَ النُّصْحَ ، وَ بَذَلَ مُهْجَتَهُ فِيكَ ، لِيَسْتَنْقِذَ عِبَادَكَ مِنَ الْجَهَالَةِ ، وَ حَيْرَةِ الضَّلَالَةِ ، وَ قَدْ تَوَازَرَ عَلَيْهِ مَنْ غَرَّتْهُ الدُّنْيَا ، وَ بَاعَ حَظَّهُ بِالْأَرْذَلِ الْأَدْنَى ، وَ شَرَى آخِرَتَهُ بِالثَّمَنِ الْأَوْكَسِ ، وَ تَغَطْرَسَ وَ تَرَدَّى فِي هَوَاهُ ، وَ أَسْخَطَ نَبِيَّكَ ، وَ أَطَاعَ مِنْ عِبَادِكَ أَهْلَ الشِّقَاقِ وَ النِّفَاقِ ، وَ حَمَلَةَ الْأَوْزَارِ الْمُسْتَوْجِبِينَ النَّارَ ، فَجَاهَدَهُمْ فِيكَ صَابِراً مُحْتَسِباً ، حَتَّى سُفِكَ فِي طَاعَتِكَ دَمُهُ ، وَ اسْتُبِيحَ حَرِيمُهُ ، اَللَّهُمَّ فَالْعَنْهُمْ لَعْناً وَبِيلًا ، وَ عَذِّبْهُمْ عَذَاباً أَلِيماً

اَلسَّلَامُ عَلَيْكَ يَا ابْنَ رَسُولِ اللهِ ، اَلسَّلَامُ عَلَيْكَ يَا ابْنَ سَيِّدِ الْأَوْصِيَاءِ ، أَشْهَدُ أَنَّكَ أَمِينُ اللهِ وَ ابْنُ أَمِينِهِ ، عِشْتَ سَعِيداً وَ مَضَيْتَ حَمِيداً ، وَ مِتَّ فَقِيداً مَظْلُوماً شَهِيداً ، وَ أَشْهَدُ أَنَّ اللهَ مُنْجِزٌ مَا وَعَدَكَ ، وَ مُهْلِكٌ مَنْ خَذَلَكَ ، وَ مُعَذِّبٌ مَنْ قَتَلَكَ ، وَ أَشْهَدُ أَنَّكَ وَفَيْتَ بِعَهْدِ اللهِ ، وَ جَاهَدْتَ فِي سَبِيلِهِ حَتَّى أَتَاكَ الْيَقِينُ ، فَلَعَنَ اللهُ مَنْ قَتَلَكَ ، وَ لَعَنَ اللهُ مَنْ ظَلَمَكَ ، وَ لَعَنَ اللهُ أُمَّةً سَمِعَتْ بِذَلِكَ فَرَضِيَتْ بِهِ

اَللَّهُمَّ إِنِّي أُشْهِدُكَ أَنِّي وَلِيٌّ لِمَنْ وَالَاهُ ، وَ عَدُوٌّ لِمَنْ عَادَاهُ ، بِأَبِي أَنْتَ وَ أُمِّي يَا ابْنَ رَسُولِ اللهِ ، أَشْهَدُ أَنَّكَ كُنْتَ نُوراً فِي الْأَصْلَابِ الشَّامِخَةِ ، وَ الْأَرْحَامِ الطَّاهِرَةِ ، لَمْ تُنَجِّسْكَ الْجَاهِلِيَّةُ بِأَنْجَاسِهَا ، وَ لَمْ تُلْبِسْكَ الْمُدْلَهِمَّاتُ مِنْ ثِيَابِهَا ، وَ أَشْهَدُ أَنَّكَ مِنْ دَعَائِمِ الدِّينِ ، وَ أَرْكَانِ الْمُسْلِمِينَ ، وَ مَعْقِلُ الْمُؤْمِنِينَ ، وَ أَشْهَدُ أَنَّكَ الْإِمَامُ الْبَرُّ التَّقِيُّ الرَّضِيُّ الزَّكِيُّ الْهَادِي الْمَهْدِيُّ ، وَ أَشْهَدُ أَنَّ الْأَئِمَّةَ مِنْ وُلْدِكَ ، كَلِمَةُ التَّقْوَى ، وَ أَعْلَامُ الْهُدَى ، وَ الْعُرْوَةُ الْوُثْقَى ، وَ الْحُجَّةُ عَلَى أَهْلِ الدُّنْيَا ، وَ أَشْهَدُ أَنِّي بِكُمْ مُؤْمِنٌ ، وَ بِإِيَابِكُمْ مُوقِنٌ ، بِشَرَائِعِ دِينِي ، وَ خَوَاتِيمِ عَمَلِي ، وَ قَلْبِي لِقَلْبِكُمْ سِلْمٌ ، وَ أَمْرِي لِأَمْرِكُمْ مُتَّبِعٌ ، وَ نُصْرَتِي لَكُمْ مُعَدَّةٌ ، حَتَّى يَأْذَنَ اللهُ لَكُمْ ، فَمَعَكُمْ مَعَكُمْ ، لَا مَعَ عَدُوِّكُمْ ، صَلَوَاتُ اللهِ عَلَيْكُمْ ، وَ عَلَى أَرْوَاحِكُمْ وَ أَجْسَادِكُمْ ، وَ شَاهِدِكُمْ وَ غَائِبِكُمْ ، وَ ظَاهِرِكُمْ وَ بَاطِنِكُمْ ، آمِينَ رَبَّ الْعَالَمِينَ

Transliteration of Arbaeen Ziyarah

ASSALAAMO A'LAA WALIYYILLAAHE WA HABEEBEHI..
ASSALAAMO A'LAA KHALEELILLAAHE WA NAJEEBEHI
ASSALAAMO A'LAA SAFIYYILLAAHE WABNA SAFIYYEHI
ASSALAAMO A'LAL HUSYANIL MAZLOOMISH SHAHEEDE
ASAAALAAMO A'LAA ASEERIL KOROBAATE WA QATEELIL A'BARAATE
ALLAAHUMMAA INNEE ASH-HADO ANNAHU WALIYYOKA WABNO WALIYYEKA WA SAFIYYOKA WABNO SAFIYYEKAL...
FAAA-EZO BE-KARAAMATEKA AKRAMTAHU BISH SHAHAADATE WA
HABAWTAHU BIS SA-A'DATE WAJ-TABAYTAHU BE-TEEBIL WELAADATE WA JA-A'LTAHU SAYYEDAN MENAS SAADATE WA QAAA-EDAN MENAL QAADATE WA ZAAA-EDAN MINAZ ZAADATE WA
AA'-TAYTAHU MAWAAREESUL AMBEYAAA-E WA JA-A'LTAHU HUJJATAN A'LAA KHALQEKA MENAL AWSEYAAA-E FA-AA'-ZARA FIDDO-AAA-E WA MANAHAN NUSHA WA BAZALA MOHJATAHU FEEKA LE-
YASTANQEZA E'BAADEKA MENAL JAHAALATI WA HAYRATIZ ZALAALATE WA QAD TAWAAZARA A'LAYHE MAN GHARRAT-HUD DUNYAA WA BAA-A' HAZZAHU BIL-ARZALIL ADNAA WA SHARAA AAKHERATAHU BIS-SAMANIL AWKASE WA TA-GHAT-RASA WA...
TARADDAA FEE HAWAAHO WA ASKHATAKA WA ASKHATA NABIYYAKA

*WA ATAA-A' MIN E'BAADEKA AHLASH SHEQAAQE WAN NEFAAQE
WA
HAMALATAL AWZAARIL MUSTAWJEBEENAN NAARA FA-JAAHADA
HUM FEEKA SAABERAN MOHTASEBAN HATTAA SOFEKA FEE TAA-
A'TEKA DAMOHU WASTOBEEHA HAREEMOHU ALLAAHUMMA
FALA'NHUM LA'-NAN WABEELAN WA A'ZZIBHUM A'ZAABAN
ALEEMAN...
ASSALAAMO A'LAYKA YABNA RASOOLILLAAHE
ASSALAAMO A'LAYKA YABNA SAYYEDIL AWSEYAAA-E ASH-HADO
ANNAKA AMEENULLAAHE WABNO AMEENEHI I'SHTA SA-E'EDAN
WA
MAZAYTA HAMEEDAN WA MUTTA FAQEEDAN MAZLOOMAN
SHAHEEDAN ....
WA ASH-HADO ANNALLAAHA MUNJEZUN MAA WA-A'DAKA WA
MOHLEKUN MAN KHAZALAKA WA MO-A'ZZEBUN MAN
QATALAKA WA
ASH-HADO ANNAKA WAFAYTA BE-A'HDILLAAHE WA JAAHADTA
FEESABEELEHI HATTAA AATAYRKAL YAQEENO FA-LA-
A'NALLAAHO MAN
QATALAKA WA LA-A'NALLAAHO MAN ZALAMAKA WA LA-
A'NALLAAHO UMMATAN SAME-A'T BE-ZAALEKA FARAZEYAT BEHI
..
ALLAHUMA INNEE USH-HEDOKA ANNEE WALIYYUN LEMAN
WALAAHO
WA A'DUWWUN LEMAN A'ADAAHO BE-ABEE ANTA WA UMMEE
YABNA RASOOLILLAAHE ASH-HADO ANNAAKA KUNTA NOORAN*

FILASLAABISH SHAAMEKHATE WAL ARHAAMIL MOTAHHARATE LAM TONAJJISKAL JAAHELIYYATO BE-ANJAASEHAA WA LAM TULBISKAL
MUDLAHIMMAATO MIN SEYAABEHAA WA ASH-HADO ANNAKA MIN DAA'AA-EMID DEENE WA ARKAANIL MUSLEMEENA WA MA'-QELIL MOMINEENA WA ASH-HADO ANNAKAL EMAAMUL BARRUT TAQQIYYUR RAZIYYUZ ZAKIYYUL HAADIL MAHDIYYO WA ASH-HADO ANNAL A-IMMATA MIN WULDEKA KALEMATUT TAQWAA WA AA'-LAAMUL
HODAA WAL U'RWATUL WUSQAA WAL HUJJATO A'LAA AHLID DUNYAA WA ASH-HADO ANNEE BEKUM MO-MENUN WA BE-EYAABEKUM MOOQENUN BE-SHARAA-YE-E'DEENEE WA KHAWAATEEME A'MALEE WA QALBEE LE-QALBEKUM SILMUN WA AMREE LE-AMREKUM MUTTABE-U'N WA NUSRATEE LAKUM MO-A'DDATUN HATTAA YAAZANALLAAHO LUKUM FA-MA-A'KUM LAA MA-A' A'DDUWWEKUM SALAWAATULLAAHE A'LAYKUM
WA A'LAA ARWAAHEKUM WA AJSAADEKUM WA SHAAHEDEKUM WAGHAAA-EBEKUM WA ZAAHEREKUM WA BAATENEKUM AAMEENA RABBAL A'ALAAMEENA ...

Translation of Arbaeen Ziyarah

'Peace be on the favorite of Allah, peace be on the beloved friend of Allah, His distinguished hero. Peace be on the choicest confidant of Allah, sincerely attached precisely like his father. Peace be on Hussain, who gave his life in the way of Allah, a martyr, underwent untold hardships Peace be on the hostage surrounded by the-tightening circle of sorrow and grief, killed by a horde of savages.

O my Allah I give witness that beyond a shadow of doubt he is Thy favorite and choicest confidant, who enjoys Thy confidence and favor, precisely like his father! Thou looked up to him and elected him in Thy cause, picked and chose him for the good fortune, selected for him the best purified parents, appointed him guardian, leader, and defender of rights, a true representative (inheritor and progenitor) of guardians, leaders and defenders of rights, gave him much and more from the inheritance of the Prophets, put him forward as a decisive argument, along with the other successors (of the Holy Prophet-the twelve lmams) to the mankind.

He met with deadly dangers, acted justly and fairly, made use of everything belonging to him to pay full attention to give sincere advice, took pains, made every effort and put his heart, mind, soul and life at the disposal of Thy mission to liberate the people from the yoke of ignorance and evil of bewilderment, but an evildoer, deceived with empty hopes of mean and worthless worldly gains, had pressed heavily on him, and sold out his share (eternal bliss) for the meanest and lowest bargain, betrayed his "day of judgment" for a vulgar return, took pride in insolence, fell into the fathom- well of silly stupid follies, provoked Thee and Thy Prophet to anger, did as the harsh discordant, the hypocrite, the heavily burdened bearers of sin, condemned to Hellfire, advised to him, however, he (the Holy lmam), steadily, rightly and justly coped With them, till, in Thy obedience, gave his life after which his family was set adrift. O my Allah, therefore, condemn them to hell as a denunciation and conviction; and crack-down on them with a painful Punishment.

Peace be on you O the son of the Messenger of Allah! Peace be on you O the son of the first of the successors (of the Holy Prophet)! I bear witness that Allah put faith in you like He had full confidence in your father, and that you always looked for and collected good and virtue, lived a highly praiseworthy life and departed from this world a martyr, forsaken and abused; I bear witness that Allah will promptly fulfill the promise, He made to you, and destroy those who left you helpless and punish those who killed you; I bear witness that you kept your promise made with Allah, and strived in His way till what was certain came upon you, so curse of Allah be an those who killed you, curse of Allah be on those who oppressed you, curse of Allah be on the people who came to know and approved.

O my Allah be my witness that I make friends with those who love him and oppose those who deny him. I, my father and mother, are at your disposal oh the son of the Messenger of Allah. I know and bear witness that you were "light" in the sublime loins and in the pure wombs, never touched you the dirt of ignorance, nor ever obscurity concealed you in its folds; I bear witness that you are the pillar of "Deen", support of the Muslims, refuge of the faithful; I bear witness that you are a truthful, well-aware, content, intelligent, rightly guided guide (Imam); I bear witness that the Imams among your descendants are the symbols of "conscious piety" and signs of "true guidance", the "safe handle"-Islam, and the decisive arguments over mankind; I declare positively that I have full faith in you and I know for certain that you shall return. I am, fully committed to the laws of my religion, certain of my deeds, my mind and heart ready for your return, and my affairs carried out in the light of your instructions, till Allah gives you permission, together with you, along with you, not at the same time with your enemies. Blessings of Allah be on you, on your souls, on your bodies when you are visible, when you are invisible, on your perceivable aspects, on your innermost genius be it so, O Lord of the worlds.

Bibliography

Al-Amili, A., *Wasa'il Al-Shia*, Dar Ihyaa Al-Turath Al-Arabi, Beirut, 1983.

Al-Amudi, A., *Ghurar Al-Hikam*, Dar Al-Huda Publications, Beirut, 1995.

Al-Harani, H., *Tuhaf Al-Uqool*, Al-Alami Publications, Beirut, 2010.

Al-Haythami, N.A., *Majma' Al-Zawa'id*, Maktabat Al-Qudsi, Cairo, 1994.

Al-Hilli, J.A., *Kashf Al-Murad fe Sharh Tajreed Al-Iqtiqad*, Al-Alami Publications, Beirut, 1995.

Al-Hilli, Y.A., *Mujama' Al-Buhooth Al-Islamia*, Qum (no date)

Al-Hindi, M., *Kanz al-Ummal fe Sunan Al-Aqwal wal Af'aal*, Bait Al-Afkar Al-Dawliya, Riyadh, 2005.

Al-Kulayni, S.M., *Usul Al-Kafi*, Manshourat Al-Fajr, Beirut, 2007.

Al-Maghribi, A. A., *Da'aim Al-Islam*, Dar Al-Ma'arif, Cairo, 1963.

Al-Majlisi, M.B., *Bihar Al-Anwar*, Mu'assasat Ihya Al-Kutub Al-Islamiyya, Qum, 2008.

Al-Mashhadi, M., *Al-Mazar Al-Kabir*, Mu'assasat Al-Nashr Al-Islami, Qum, 1997.

Al-Mufid, S.M., *Kitab Al-Irshad*, Ansariyan Publications, Qum, 2004.

Al-Muqarram, A., *Maqtal Al-Hussain*, Al-Shareef Al-Radhi Publications, Beirut, 1998.

Al-Murtadha, S., *Al-Dharee'a ila Wusul Al-Sharee'a*, Tehran University Publications, 1988.

Al-Musawi, T.A., *Marqad Imam Al-Hussain abr al-tarikh*, Dar Al-Fiqh, Qum, 1421AH.

Al-Najafi, M.H., *Jawahir Al-Kalam fe Sharh Shara' Al-Islam*, Dar Ihyaa Al-Turath Al-Arabi, Beirut, 1981. Fourth edition

Al-Nouri, M.H., *Mustadrak Al-Wasa'il*, Mu'assasat Alulbayt le Ihyaa Al-Turath, Qum, 1991.

Al-Qummi, A., *Manazil Al-Akhira*, Mu'asassat Al-Balagh, Beirut, 2007.

Al-Qummi, A., *Mafatih Al-Jinan*, Dar Al-Adhwa, Beirut, 1422AH.

Al-Qurtubi, M., *al-Jami' li-ahkam-il-Qur'an (Tafsir Al-Qurtubi)*, accessed via altafsir.com on 9 October 2016.

Al-Radhi, A., *Nahjul Balagha*, Dar Al-Kitab, Beirut, 1429AH.

Al-Razi, F.A., *Tafsir Al-Kabir*, Dar Ihya Al-Turath Al-Arabi, Beirut, 1420AH.

Al-Sabaki, T.A. *Tabaqat al-Shaf'iya al-Kubra*, Faisal Al-Halabi Publications, 1964.

Al-Saduq M., *Amali Al-Saduq*, Al-Alami Publications, Beirut, 2001.

Al-Saduq, M., *Ilal Al-Shara'i, Dar Al-Murathda*, Beirut, 2013.

Al-Saduq, S.M., *Man La Yahthrahu Al-Faqih, Mu'assasat Al-A'lami*, 1986 First Edition.

Al-Saffar, M.H., *Basa'ir Al-Darajat*, Al-Alami Publications, Beirut, 2003.

Al-Shirazi, N.M., *Al-Amthal fe Tafsir Kitab Allah Al-Munzal*, Madrasat Imam Ali, Qum, 1426AH.

Al-Simyani, H., *Al-Arbaeen wa falsafatul Mashee ila Hussain*, Imam Hussain shrine publications, 2015.

Al-Tabari, M., *Tareekh Al-Tabari, Mu'assasat Al-A'lami*, Beirut, 1998.

Al-Tabarsi, A.M., *Al-Ihtijaj*, Dar Al-Uswa, Iran, 1989.

Al-Tirmidhi, M., *Sunan Al-Tirmidhi*, www.ahadith.co.uk, accessed 13 June 2017.

Al-Tusi, M., *A'mali Al-Tusi, Dar Al-Kutub Al-Islamiya*, Iran, 1414AH.

Al-Tusi, S.M., *Tahdhib Al-ahkam*, Dar Al-Kutub Al-Islamiyya, Tehran, 1970.

Al-Yazdi, M.K., *Al-Urwat Al-Wuthqa*, Mu'asassat Maytham Al-Tammar, Najaf, 2009.

Bukhari, M., *Sahih Bukhari*, www.ahadith.co.uk, accessed 13 June 2017.

Ibn Hanbal, A. *Fadhail Al-Sahaba*, Mu'asassat Al-Risalah, Beirut, 1983.

Ibn Hanbal, A., *Musnad Al-Imam Ahmed ibn Hanbal*, Dar Al-Minhaj, Jeddah, 2008.

Ibn Kathir, *Al-Bidaya wal Nihaya*, Maktabat Al-Ma'arif, Beirut, 1990.

Ibn Manthur, *Lisan Al-Arab*, Dar Saader, Beirut, 1414AH.

Ibn Tawus, S. A., *Al-Luhuf ala Qatla Al-Tufuf*, Dar Al-Uswa, 1992.

Ibne Quluwayh, J.M.M., *Kamilul Al-Ziyarat*, Al-Serat Publications, Mumbai, 2010.

Muslim, I., *Sahih Muslim*, Dar Tayba, Riyadh, 2006.

Sistani, A., *Minhaj Al-Saleehen*, Dar Al-Mu'rakh Al-Arabi, Beirut, 2008.

Tusi, M. H., *Misbah Al-Mutahajid*, Al-A'lami Publications, Beirut, 1998.

About the Author

Sheikh Mohammed Al-Hilli is an Islamic scholar and speaker who has visited and presented lectures in many parts of the world, from Africa to Australia and from the US, Canada to Europe. He has a Masters in Pharmacy from the University of London and an MA in Islamic Studies from Middlesex University in the UK. For over 10 years, Sheikh Al-Hilli studied Hawza (Islamic Seminary education) in London and Najaf. He is a teacher for Hawza studies at the Islamic College in London. He is currently head of Islamic Education Department at Noor Trust in the UK, conducting Quranic commentary programmes, marriage workshops as well as youth activities.

Sheikh Al-Hilli has taken part in the Najaf to Karbala Arbaeen walk annually since 2012 with the Spiritual Journeys Ziyarah group.

Notes